Praise *Innovate Inside the Box*

"*Innovate Inside the Box* is a hard-headed guide to infusing innovation into the classroom. Couros and Novak show how to adopt an Innovator's Mindset—and then offer page after page of intriguing ideas and catalysts for action. If you're looking to bring creativity to student learning amid all the constraints educators face, this is the book for you."

–Daniel Pink, author of *When*, *Drive*, and *A Whole New Mind*

"No one articulates a more compelling, a more urgent, or a more motivating vision of education—for both teachers and their students—than George Couros. No one articulates how that vision can be reached—for every student and teacher—more daringly, more practically, and more inclusively, than Katie Novak. Having them together in one book not only helps us reimagine the goals and practices of education, it reminds us of why we ever wanted to be teachers at all."

–David Rose, PhD, CAST's cofounder and chief education officer, emeritus

"An incredible book! *Innovate Inside the Box* speaks to educators who are the change agents in their sphere of influence. The insights from Novak and Couros, provided through relatable anecdotes and multiple opportunities to reflect, make this book a valuable resource for readers who are seeking to 'be the [proverbial] change.'"

–Sarah Thomas, PhD, founder of EduMatch

"George and Katie's combined talents as spectacular storytellers drive this book. You will feel like you are flying through it and then realize how deeply you are learning. Both share the 'stage' well as they intertwine the Core of Innovative Teaching and Learning, the Characteristics of an Innovator's Mindset, and Universal Design for Learning. You will leave the pages feeling inspired, motivated, and restored."

–Loui Lord Nelson, PhD, author of *Design and Deliver* and podcast host of *UDL in 15 Minutes*

W9-ARO-832

"Couros and Novak do an amazing job addressing the reality of constraints in education that we face. They share opportunities and ideas of how to overcome those barriers and *Innovate Inside the Box* we are given. This is a thought-provoking book I didn't want to put down, which left me feeling inspired and empowered. This is a must read if you are in any way involved with education."

–Pam Erickson, elementary teacher, ISD 97

"As a fan of *Innovator's Mindset,* I knew that it would be hard to follow up with another book, but I was blown away by how inspirational this book was and how it provides practical ideas on how to lead meaningful change within the constraints of our systems. *Innovate Inside the Box* is both inspiring and filled with practical, real-world examples of how to empower learners to do amazing things while they are still in school that will develop our students as both the leaders of today and tomorrow."

–A.J. Juliani, author of *Empower* and *The PBL Playbook*

"A thoughtful and kind approach to innovation in education. It reads as more of a conversation than an evaluation of modern learning with a mix of inspiring yet vulnerable stories and practical ideas that can make an immediate difference with all learners. *Innovate Inside the Box* is the type of book that hits the sweet spot of making me uncomfortable while validating much of my path. I could not put this book down."

–Meghan Lawson, coordinator of instructional services, Hamilton County Educational Service Center

"Masterful! Couros and Novak have woven together a collection of timeless stories and practitioner-friendly insights that make innovation more accessible than ever before. *Innovate Inside the Box* contains a heartfelt array of resources that will stretch and affirm you, regardless of the position you're serving in. The relational underpinnings of innovative teaching and learning are on full display in this rare read, so much so that this book is sure to captivate and encourage generations of educators moving forward."

–**Brad Gustafson**, principal at Wayzata Public Schools, author of *Renegade Leadership* and *Reclaiming Our Calling*

"A wonderful conversational union of Innovator's Mindset, UDL, and the practicality of HOW to shift your classroom and school's environment. George and Katie walking through each characteristic of the Innovator's Mindset using a UDL lens really blew my mind! Specific examples of how and why to do things to truly innovate your own mindset as well as your learners! This is a must read for folks who are interested in UDL!"

–**Lizzie Fortin**, instructional coach/visual art teacher, Worcester Public Schools

'*The Innovator's Mindset* changed my trajectory as a teacher, so my expectations for *Innovate Inside the Box* seemed unrealistically high. It should come as no surprise, however, that my expectations were far exceeded. This book not only touches your heart, but Novak and Couros also provide countless meaningful ideas for teaching in a way that makes you feel as though they are exploring with you instead of telling you what to do. Every educator, no matter their role, needs to read this book."

–**Annick Rauch**, grade 1 French immersion teacher, learner, mom

"Couros and Novak address a fundamental problem prevalent in education today: Our systems move so slowly that we need, and have the power, to innovate inside the box! They challenge the reader to identify how to make a positive impact while understanding the obstacles we face and emphasize ways to be truly learner-centered. They state, '. . . we must help students develop a learner orientation so they can see a deeper meaning to the learning that is happening within their school experience and take it with them wherever they choose to go. And that kind of learning requires innovative, learner-driven, evidence-informed teaching.' This is one of the most powerful statements in the book and one of many that will resonate with all readers!"

–Dwight Carter, Eastland Career Center
assistant director, leadership coach

"Truly exceptional! George Couros and Katie Novak wrote something masterful with *Innovate Inside the Box*. As a follow-up to the best-selling book *Innovators Mindset*, they drive home the importance of focusing on nurturing the learner. Too often, we get stuck on trying to 'fix' students' deficiencies, struggles, and weaknesses rather than nurturing their talents, strengths, ideas, and the individual gifts they bring to the classroom. This book is thought-provoking and practical for both teachers and school leaders and is definitely a book I will be recommending to others."

–Jimmy Casas, educator, speaker, leadership coach

"As leaders in learner mindsets and UDL, George and Katie have joined forces to share characteristics and actions that focus on students—not as pawns for schools to use to attain higher state standings, but as people that we, as educators, strive to help reach their potential inside the classroom and beyond. While the ideas they present are research based, they have written them in a conversational tone that makes for an enjoyable reading experience. I am positive that, whether read as part of a group book study or individually, the reader will finish this book happy to realize that future interactions with students will be different because of it."

–Josh Underwood, Presidential Award for Excellence
in Mathematics and Science Teaching recipient and
Kentucky High School teacher of the year

"In *Innovate Inside the Box*, Couros and Novak brilliantly fuse together key aspects of the Innovator's Mindset and UDL Principles and offer a deep dive into their *"Core of Innovative Teaching and Learning"* to provide readers with practical strategies to ensure learner-centered, evidence-driven experiences, while simultaneously tackling difficult issues plaguing educators today. The authors provide tangible catalysts for action that can be implemented in your school or classroom the following day. Brilliantly written, this book will challenge your mindset and inspire you to continue moving forward for those we serve."

–Thomas C. Murray, director of innovation,
Future Ready Schools,® Washington, DC

"It is with great pleasure that I endorse this book. It offers something for all educators, from preschool to higher education. While I appreciate what every chapter has to offer, I especially appreciate the emphasis on relationships. As a higher-education instructor located in a developing country, oftentimes when I read education books, I find them filled with information that may not always apply to my setting. That is not the case with this book, as it offers, in every chapter and in the form of questions and tips, specific and clearly stated suggestions about instilling a UDL-infused innovator's mindset in one's students and oneself. The questions that are part of every chapter are especially helpful as they make one truly think about one's role as an educator. This book has offered me numerous and innovative ways of creating change 'within the box.'"

–Lara El Khatib, professor, American
Lebanese University, Lebanon

"Honest and actionable, *Innovate Inside the Box* connects a concept that every designer knows and that every educator needs to know *and embrace*: constraints. Every designer has to work within constraints, and Couros and Novak acknowledge this in a simple but powerful statement for educators: Stop waiting for the system to change. Testing, grades, and standardization aren't going anywhere in our lifetime, and Couros and Novak set this up as the box. From the onset, *Innovate* fuses the characteristics of the innovator's mindset and Universal Design for Learning through personal examples and implementation strategies tested by innovative leaders and educators in the field, while preserving the distinct voices of Couros and Novak educators have come to value and anticipate. Every educator who picks up this book will find themselves affirmed, challenged, and equipped to *Innovate Inside the Box*!"

–**Joni Degner**, consultant and designer at DTour, UDL facilitator, Bartholomew Consolidated School Corporation

"The premise of Innovate Inside the Box is immediately intriguing and exactly what educational designers need. Often, educators are stuck in the position of wanting to create change in dystopic systems but are either constrained by the sheer size of the system or knowing where to start. Innovate Inside the Box offers practical insight and application into changing current education through continual small disruptions that have big payoffs. It is a beautiful amalgamation of UDL concepts and innovator mindsets. I wish I had this guidebook as a starting place in systems design."

–**Bryan Dean**, instructional designer, Universal Design for Learning integrationist, guerrilla teacher

INNOVATE
INSIDE the
BOX

Empowering Learners Through UDL and the Innovator's Mindset

George Couros with Katie Novak

Innovate Inside the Box
© 2019 by George Couros with Katie Novak

All rights reserved. No part of this publication may be reproduced in any form or by any electronic or mechanical means, including information storage and retrieval systems, without permission in writing by the publisher, except by a reviewer who may quote brief passages in a review. For information regarding permission, contact the publisher at books@impressbooks.org.

This book is available at special discounts when purchased in quantity for use as premiums, promotions, fundraisers, or for educational use. For inquiries and details, contact the publisher at books@impressbooks.org.

Published by IMPRESS, a division of Dave Burgess Consulting, Inc.
ImpressBooks.org
daveburgessconsulting.com

Library of Congress Control Number: 2019946508
Paperback ISBN: 978-1-948334-12-9
eBook ISBN: 978-1-948334-13-6

First Printing: August 2019

DEDICATION

From George

To my daughter, Kallea. This book is focused on how we can help kids change the world for the better, but you made my world better the moment you entered my life. I love you, and I am proud of you. Thank you for being the bright light in my life.

From Katie

Torin, Aylin, Brec, and Boden. Always remember our two rules for you: Be nice and work hard. In short, the Innovator's Mindset can be summed up there. Never forget the power of either. Now, choose something to fight for and go out and change the world. Love, Momma.

CONTENTS

FOREWORD
by Katie Martin
author of *Learner-Centered Innovation*

I met George in 2014, when he spoke at the University of San Diego where I worked as director of professional learning. We had an opportunity to connect before he spoke, and I shared some of what we were learning from our research and how we were supporting educators to shift practice and more effectively use technology. In his own special style (which I continue to appreciate), George validated and pushed my thinking in a way I had never experienced. That day, he encouraged me to write something on my whiteboard that hung next to my computer. It was a question and not-so-subtle nudge that changed me forever: "How can you make great learning go viral?"

George knew that connecting with others was critical to my own growth and my impact on learners. I have always been passionate about creating new and better learning environments as a teacher and have always learned so much every time I worked with students, teachers, administrators, and families or visited classrooms, but I kept much of this to myself. Up until this conversation with George, I had post-it notes and documents of all my ideas safely tucked away in my office. Periodically, I would revisit and reformat these ideas and possibly add more citations to validate my ideas or try things with a few schools that I was working with, but I never thought that my ideas and successes were quite perfect enough to share more broadly, and so I didn't.

I had convinced myself that the strategies I found so successful and the professional learning experiences that I had been leading were similar to what others were already doing. Even when I saw great success and impact on educators and students, I never believed they were quite good enough to share. At the same time, I often felt that some of my ideas were way too grandiose and never truly possible. I have always been passionate about ensuring that students have opportunities to build on their own strengths and interests. I also believe that educators need the same kinds of opportunities to create new and better experiences for their students. As I connected with educators, I discovered that others shared my dreams and beliefs about education.

But, like many educators, I had been paralyzed by the notion of perfection. My own fears had prevented me from achieving the goals about which I was so passionate. George pushed me to share (as he has done for so many educators) because he believed that others could benefit from my ideas and that I could learn from the feedback that others would provide. What quickly became apparent to me was that learners in our education system would ultimately reap the benefits of our collective growth.

I have grown exponentially in my professional life in the past years because I have been more open about my ideas and have connected with educators around the world who have pushed and expanded my thinking about what is possible in our schools today. As I continue to learn and evolve, I know that I have to model the same practices that I hope to see educators model and practice in their classrooms and be open to learning from success and failure. To be perfectly honest, I still struggle every time I teach a class or lead professional learning and wonder if my ideas will resonate or if the experiences I have designed are the right ones. It takes courage to show up and be vulnerable, and I constantly channel Brené Brown, who says, "Vulnerability is the birthplace of innovation, creativity and change." Because I have experienced the benefit and know how it has helped me improve and grow, I continue to put myself out there and test my ideas.

Why Innovation in Education Is Critical

Visiting more than 500 classrooms across the world has provided me insight into the tremendous shifts in education. It's inspiring to see educators who are looking to their learners, ensuring relationships are the core, continually learning to evolve in their practice, making evidence-informed decisions, and creating empowering learning experiences based on the needs of the learners. I have also noticed the discrepancy in the range of access and opportunities kids have in schools. As I am encouraged to see more and more learner-centered practices, I also feel a sense of urgency to make these experiences and environments the norm throughout education for all children.

The challenge I see in classrooms and hear about in conversations with students, teachers, administrators, and families is that there is misalignment between our aspirations—what we believe that learners need—and what we actually do in schools. Too often, our past practices and mindsets about change prevent us from developing learner-centered experiences aligned with our vision. I get it. The potential cost of failure feels far more risky and potentially damaging than managing the status quo. The more I think about this though, the more I realize that failure is what happens when we allow zip codes to predict test scores and student engagement and motivation to decline rapidly the longer kids are in school. The fact that the tutoring industry outside of the school day is a goldmine is an indication that, although students want to learn and prepare for their future, they are increasingly ill-prepared for the workforce, underemployed, or just plain lost when it comes to life after school. It's also evidence that the high-stakes standardized accountability systems in our schools are at odds with authentic learning.

To redefine success, we also have to define what it really means to fail. If we were really afraid of failing our students and our communities, we would be relentless about looking at the learners we serve, evolving our pedagogical practices, and creating the systems and policies that support a more holistic view of success that aligns with the world we live in and ridding them of ones that impede authentic learning, growth, and innovation.

Educators are working harder than ever, but I wonder if sometimes we are getting better at the wrong things. Our system was designed for a different era where standardization was the goal and, as a result, is not intended to develop the skills our students need to be successful today. Changing the education system can seem daunting if we focus on all the barriers, but then we must remind ourselves that it was designed by people. The Committee of 10 (in 1892) created the rules that reflected the values of the late 1800s and designed a system to prepare learners for an industrial era. Our world and our needs have changed, and will continue to, and the only way to change the system is through people who believe in themselves and our collective future enough to make the changes that are necessary today. That means you are part of the solution, and that is why we must innovate inside the box.

The Opportunities Ahead

In George's first book, *The Innovator's Mindset*, he helped us see that innovation is needed because our world, and the learners we serve, demand new and different learning experiences. If we understand that the system, as it's currently designed, cannot fully meet the needs of all learners, we have to also understand that the status quo will never enable all learners to reach their full potential.

Innovate Inside the Box continues the conversation by focusing on creating opportunities for kids to develop the skills and motivation to solve problems in their day-to-day lives and engage in our global world. Many of today's kids will have to *create* their jobs and forge a new path. Yes, we need to teach foundational skills; knowing how to read and write is critical, but possessing these skills cannot be the end goal. Ultimately, we must ensure we remove the barriers and provide opportunities for all students to develop foundational skills and use their knowledge to communicate, collaborate, and solve meaningful problems. When we tell learners to complete an assignment, we get compliance. When we empower learners to investigate and make an impact on the world, we inspire problem-solvers and innovators.

This book's co-author, Katie Novak, notes that "Learners are not disabled. Curriculum is. Systems are. But kids are not." With that in mind, she shares how Universal Design For Learning (UDL) acts as a framework that helps us find new and better ways to teach the required standards and objectives. This framework empowers us to engage learners, represent content and ideas in multiple ways, and provide learners with voice and choice regarding how they express what they know.

The power of *Innovate Inside the Box* is that it combines the characteristics of the "Innovator's Mindset" with UDL to help us cast a broader vision of success than test scores. This vision encompasses skills that are critical for

> **When we empower learners to investigate and make an impact on the world, we inspire problem-solvers and innovators.**

learners to develop to thrive in our world today. George pushes us to see what is possible, while validating essential components of effective teaching and learning (like building relationships). He urges us to see all learners for the wondrous, capable, and unique individuals they are. Katie provides targeted strategies aligned to UDL principles to help us create learning experiences and environments that spark curiosity, ignite passion, and unleash genius.

George and Katie address the barriers all educators face, such as time, resources, and testing requirements. They also show us what's possible and how many teachers are leveraging the Innovator's Mindset to find new and better ways to serve their students inside these common constraints.

Throughout this book you will be validated for the great things you are already doing. You will also be pushed to think about how you can recognize, honor, and build on the unique strengths and talents you, your colleagues, and your students possess. Most importantly of all, you will be inspired to put your ideas into action.

Wherever you are in your journey, George and Katie's collective expertise and accessible ideas will motivate you to take the next step. Ultimately it is up to you to imagine what is possible in your context, connect with others, try your new ideas, and figure out what works best for you and the learners you serve. As you navigate this journey, please know that your ideas, experiences, and even your failures are valuable to us all. As George taught me, when you share, we are all better for it.

Onward.

BECAUSE OF A TEACHER

It doesn't matter who you are, where you come from. The ability to triumph begins with you—always.

–Oprah Winfrey

Have you ever read an article or book that starts off by listing people who are successful in spite of their experience in school? As the son of a Greek mother, my well-used guilt meter registers off the charts when I see those lists. I know you feel it too: the pressure to do everything you can to ensure all students are successful. The message from those guilt-inducing pieces is that your students either become successful in spite of you or fail at life because of their experience in school—in your class.

Let's turn that guilt-meter down a few notches by considering the fact that those lists, wherever you find them, typically consist of about ten people. Of course, there are more than ten people who have succeeded despite a poor (or even terrible) school experience. The truth is, *many* people have had bad experiences in school. (If you are a teacher, I guarantee that people will go out of their way to tell you about their very worst school experiences.) What those lists fail to mention is that in a world of more than seven billion people, many more people have benefitted from their school experiences *because of a teacher*, including some people who have made a tremendous impact on the world.

Do you know that Maya Angelou might not have become a world-famous writer if not for the influence of her teacher, Bertha Flowers? In her autobiography, Angelou vividly recalls what Flowers said to her:

> *"Your grandmother says you read a lot. Every chance you get," she told young Maya. "That's good, but not good enough. Words mean more than what is set down on paper. It takes the human voice to infuse them with the shades of deeper meaning." Her words struck Angelou as poetic, and their relationship grew as Flowers provided Maya with new books and heightened motivation to read.*[1]

The world would not have the incredible works of Maya Angelou if it weren't for a teacher.

Bill Gates was also influenced by an educator, a librarian in his school who helped him to discover his love of reading. It's a trait that sticks with him today, and one he hopes to ignite in others by supporting education. Gates reflects:

> *Mrs. Caffiere took me under her wing and helped make it okay for me to be a messy, nerdy boy who was reading lots of books.*
>
> *She pulled me out of my shell by sharing her love of books. She started by asking questions like, "What do*

you like to read?" and "What are you interested in?"
Then she found me a lot of books—ones that were
more complex and challenging than the Tom Swift Jr.
science fiction books I was reading at the time. For
example, she gave me great biographies she had read.
Once I'd read them, she would make the time to dis-
cuss them with me. "Did you like it?" she would ask.
"Why? What did you learn?" She genuinely listened
to what I had to say.[2]

●　●　●

If you are reading this and are in the field of education, it is very likely that someone influenced you in school as well. If you are reading this and that is not true, I am sorry. My guess is that you are in education to be the person for kids that maybe no one was for you. In my own life, I have a long list of those who influenced me, such as my elementary music teacher, Mrs. Penrose, who inspired me to get on a stage. The skills and confidence I learned from participating in school productions as a child continue to serve me as I present from much larger stages today. Another teacher, Mr. Hobbs, taught me as a high school football player that leadership was not something to which I was entitled but that came from *being* someone worth following, someone who could help others move forward in a positive manner.

Teachers and administrators were not the only people in the schools I attended who left a positive mark on my life. Mr. Rohrke, our elementary school custodian, always made time to talk to my friends and me every single day. He taught us the importance of kindness and consideration of others. I cannot remember one incident of graffiti at my elementary school. None of us would have dreamt of being so inconsiderate as to deface school property because no one wanted to put our beloved custodian in a situation where he had to do extra work. Mr. Rohrke reminded me of Ron Munsey, a night custodian at a New Hampshire school who uses the vacuum to create drawings on the carpet. The students love it, of course, and rush to their rooms each morning to see the art he creates just for them.[3]

These stories and a million others serve as reminders of the impact schools—and, more importantly, the people in our schools today—have on students. They remind us that, regardless of our titles, our number one job is to serve kids. They also remind us that students who feel valued in the present are empowered to grow now and in the future. The experience provided by the adults in schools is always the beginning of something, not the end.

> **Students who feel valued in the present are empowered to grow now and in the future.**

The way we interact with students matters! We know this. That belief is the reason quotes like this one from psychologist Urie Bronfenbrenner get shared so often on social media: "Every child needs at least one adult who is irrationally crazy about him or her." At first glance, that quote sounds great, doesn't it? We all believe that! What's not to like? Well, let's stop for a minute and do some math on the above quote:

How many years does a child spend in school?

How many adults will that child interact with in his or her school career?

Based on whatever numbers you came up with, do you really think that "one," or even five, is enough?

Me neither.

That's why my mission is to ensure that students have positive, empowering interactions with all of the adults in the building, not just a select few. It's why I talk so often about the idea of "school teacher" versus "classroom teacher." *Classroom* teachers know their content amazingly well. They are great with their current group of students. But those students who never come into their classrooms? Those students are not the classroom teachers' responsibility. Those students belong to someone else.

In contrast, *school* teachers do all of those things that classroom teachers do within their own classrooms and subject matter. But when *they* walk out of their room, every child in the school is their child. We need more school teachers, because kids need more than a "few" adults in the building who make them feel important, valued, and loved.

So *how* do we create those positive encounters—the kind that last throughout the day and, more importantly, make an impact for years to come? It starts by being intentional about the words we use and the way we follow up on them with our actions. No matter what you teach, your students aren't likely to remember every lesson, but they will remember *how* you spoke and acted toward them and how you made them feel.

There is no getting around the fact that your actions and words are so important. That's true for everyone, but if you are in education, it's something that cannot be understated or forgotten. Your words—whether harsh, inspiring, degrading, or kind—can stick with people for the rest of their lives. Don't ever forget that.

I have been blessed to have former students reach out to me, and it always leaves me humbled to know that I somehow made an impact on their lives. Those encounters and walks down memory lane are generally positive, but I remember one conversation with a former student that drove home the reality of how our words stick even when they seem to be insignificant. Before I tell you how that conversation played out, let me give you the backstory.

One year early in my teaching career, as I was working with a small group of students in my grade nine math class, a student named Kyle yelled out, for no reason, "Whatever, GEOOOORGGGEEE!" It shook me. Instead of pausing to consider what might be bothering him or why he had shown what I perceived as unprovoked disrespect for me as his teacher, I quickly went into a defensive mode. (You should know that while I pride myself on being forward-thinking, I can sometimes also be very "old school." Calling a teacher by his or her first name is not old school, and in my book, was a sign of disrespect.) I looked straight at Kyle and said, "I don't know what is going on with you today, but the day you graduate high school and you turn eighteen, you can call me George all you want. Until that day, I expect you to call me Mr. Couros." Kyle quickly apologized, I accepted, and that was the end of the conversation with no mention of it again.

At the end of that school year, I moved to another district and didn't see or hear from Kyle again until one evening almost four years later. It was a Friday night. I had gotten home around 11:30 p.m. and started playing around on my computer. At 12:03 a.m. (I will never forget the time), a message popped up on Facebook from someone I didn't recognize. It went something like this:

> "Hey, George. I don't know if you remember me, George, but my name is Kyle, George. George, I just wanted to let you know that I have graduated in June, and today is my eighteenth birthday!"

I was blown away. There were probably one hundred more words to the message, and I swear that fifty of them were "George." Kyle had been eighteen for all of three minutes. Clearly, our brief classroom encounter, one that I had forgotten about until just then, had stuck with him for four years.

I responded immediately. "Kyle! Of course, I remember you! I am dying laughing right now and can't believe you remembered that conversation. I am going to cherish this moment and this message forever. Thank you for taking the time to reach out; you have made my night!"

He responded with, "See ya, George!" I never heard from him again.

I remember Kyle's personality and his incredible sense of humor. He knew I would appreciate him taking the time to write that message, but it was also a reminder that he hadn't forgotten that one brief moment in our classroom.

The bottom line is this: What we do and say can stick with our students for years, or even a lifetime.

My constant hope is that we will all strive to be intentional about building up the learners we serve. But just like my story above reveals, there is always room for personal growth. We should always be on the lookout for ways to improve ourselves, our teaching practices, and our relationships, which brings me to the subject of professional learning (PL). And why not? Your professional learning—and mine—is the entire point of this book; in fact, the need to grow in myself is part of why I am writing this book right now.

I have heard many educators lump conferences and presentations into two categories: a warm bath or a cold shower. A warm bath is meant to make us feel good. These encouraging talks validate the incredible work that is happening in schools around the world—and there is much to share!

A cold shower, on the other hand, is meant to shock us into action, and push us to do more. My hope with this book is to offer some of both. Yes, we need to celebrate the great things happening in so many classrooms, often in spite of all of the barriers that prevent all teachers, learners, and schools from doing their best work. But we all can grow. Every single one of us, including myself.

I have so many examples I could share to point out the areas in which I need to change and grow, but I will start with just one. When I wrote *The Innovator's Mindset*, it received enormous praise and a lot of positive reviews. It felt good to be validated and to know my message—my life's work—resonated with educators around the world.

Then I got my first negative review on Amazon:

> *I love the theory behind this and the examples of people doing it. However, I would have liked to read more practical ideas of implementing it with students.*

* * *

At first, I was upset. As is typical with educators (or humans, for that matter) we can hear ninety-nine compliments on our work, and then let two short sentences of criticism derail us. We (I'm pretty sure this isn't just me) become fixated on the negative remark and try to justify our position and prove that the critic is wrong. I read that two-sentence review more than I would like to admit. Eventually, the more I read it, the more I started to agree with it and understand the person's perspective. The book wasn't meant solely for administrators and could definitely be applied to the classroom, but did I give enough examples for teachers to embody the "Innovator's Mindset" in the classroom and give students the opportunity to embody this mindset in their own learning?

I always remind people that if you want to see the effectiveness of a teacher, don't watch the teacher; watch the students and see what they do because of the teacher. So instead of shrugging off this feedback, I thought about how I could use it to move forward and make things better for education and educators. I had stressed

THE INNOVATOR'S MINDSET

Belief that abilities, intelligence, and talents are developed so that they lead to the creation of new and better ideas.

the importance of others taking risks and heeding others' feed-back. This was an opportunity to implement my own advice.

Using feedback to improve is a trait of "growth mindset." Carol Dweck's impactful research and writing on the topic of growth and fixed mindsets have made a significant impact on the attitudes and cultures of schools around the world. In their book, *The Growth Mindset Coach*, authors Annie Brock and Heather Hundley share this quote and table that really resonated with me:

> *[Carol] Dweck identified five key areas in which the actions of people of opposing mindsets often diverge: challenges, obstacles, effort, criticism, and success of others. In the fixed mindset, a response to any of the five situations typically relates to the person's desire to look smart and avoid failure; in the growth mindset the response more likely stems from the person's desire to learn and improve. Let's look at both fixed- and growth-mindset responses to each of these five situations.[4]*

Situation	Fixed Mindset	Growth Mindset
Challenges	Challenges are avoided to maintain the appearance of intelligence.	Challenges are embraced stemming from a desire to learn.
Obstacles	Giving up in the face of obstacles and setbacks is a common response.	Showing perseverance in the face of obstacles and setbacks is a common response.
Effort	Having to try or put in effort is viewed as a negative. If you have to try, you're not very smart or talented.	Doing hard work and putting in effort paves the path to achievement and success.
Criticism	Negative feedback, regardless of how constructive, is ignored.	Criticism provides important feedback that can aid in learning.
Success of Others	Other people's success is viewed as a threat and evokes feelings of insecurity or vulnerability.	Other people's success can be a source of inspiration and education.

When you look at each of the Growth Mindset examples, they are admirable and beneficial for all learners within a school community (learners being all of us, not exclusively our students). But in our world today, are those traits enough? When you look at the column "Success of Others," for example, the idea that "other people's success can be a source of inspiration and education" only matters if you do something with that inspiration. I added an extra column to help others, and myself, take that necessary next step from a Growth Mindset to an Innovator's Mindset:

Situation	Fixed Mindset	Growth Mindset	Innovator's Mindset
Challenges	Challenges are avoided to maintain the appearance of intelligence.	Challenges are embraced stemming from a desire to learn.	Challenges are sought out and seen as an opportunity for growth and development.
Obstacles	Giving up in the face of obstacles and setbacks is a common response.	Showing perseverance in the face of obstacles and setbacks is a common response.	When obstacles arise, the thinking is shifted to look for opportunities and possibilities.
Effort	Having to try or put in effort is viewed as a negative. If you have to try, you're not very smart or talented.	Doing hard work and putting in effort paves the path to achievement and success.	Hard work and effort are continuous, and we look to make time to create new solutions and ideas for growth.
Criticism	Negative feedback, regardless of how constructive, is ignored.	Criticism provides important feedback that can aid in learning.	Criticism provides important feedback which creates the opportunity to implement new and better ideas for learning from others.
Success of Others	Other people's success is viewed as a threat and evokes feelings of insecurity or vulnerability.	Other people's success can be a source of inspiration and education.	Other people's success is learned from, and something we modify and apply in our own context to create our own success.

Developing a Growth Mindset is crucial, but we can't stop there. A Growth Mindset is a stepping stone on our journey from "knowing" to "doing." Knowledge is extremely important, but doing something with your knowledge is more important than ever. There is a ton of information in the world—we are inundated with it. But simply reading, studying, and even internalizing the information doesn't change the world. It's only when we take action on what we know that we can begin to solve the challenges we face and begin to make an impact. The negative comment I received could have served as something I ignored (Fixed Mindset), something I paid attention to and learned from (Growth Mindset), or, as it did in this case, a catalyst that spurred me to create something from the feedback I received (Innovator's Mindset). We want our students to not only appreciate feedback but to apply it and move forward. We need to embody that in our own work—which is why I wrote this book.

I wanted to write something that was more targeted for the classroom, something that empowered teachers *and* students. With that in mind, I have done my best to provide ideas that act as catalysts for action, but ultimately the goal is for you to modify, remix, recreate, and apply these ideas in your own context. With the acceleration of technology and information, to write a book and pretend to know or cover it all negates the diverse contexts in which teachers teach and assumes there is one right way. That idea goes against the entire notion of the *Innovator's Mindset*, which I wrote to empower readers and create new and better ways to serve students, not simply rely on past ideas and knowledge.

One of the top concerns I hear from educators around the globe about actually *implementing* their innovative ideas concerns "the system" within which they work. Red tape, limitations, a constant lack of funds, and frustrating lack of support for all students are commonalities felt by educators the world over. The title of this book, *Innovate Inside the Box*, recognizes that those constraints exist no matter your role or location. But the system, with its rules and limitations, is never a reason not to innovate. To the contrary, the system or "box" you work within may be the very reason you *need* to innovate. No matter what constraints you're dealing with, you can still do incredible things for your students and yourself.

Constraints will always be a part of what we do in education. If you don't believe me, ask any teacher with more than twenty years of experience to tell you which year of their career their school had *soooo much money* that every request was approved. You and I know the answer. I'm not saying schools shouldn't be funded better (they should) or that educators shouldn't be paid more (they should). What I am saying is that we have two choices:

1. We can focus on what we don't have and ignore the ability we have to impact our students every day, or
2. We can shift the focus to the opportunities we do have and create new and better experiences for our students.

No one is pretending that every day is going to be easy—even if you are an innovative educator. The reality is that the length of a school day has remained basically the same since I was a student myself in the 1980s. All the while, the demands for what teachers are responsible for have grown exponentially. I'm also not suggesting that you work longer hours; you need to take care of yourself emotionally, spiritually, physically, and mentally if you are going to be able to serve your students. I am proposing that you begin to think differently about how you do things and that you look for ways to make each day meaningful and rewarding for your students and for yourself.

We all want to feel a sense of purpose in our work, but we can't count on others to create that for us. We can't even always count on people or policies to support us in our efforts to do what best serves our individual learners. The most natural response to a roadblock is to stop and turn around. I want to challenge you to *Innovate Inside the Box* instead. Rather than backing up or stalling out, look for another way around the problem. Your final solution may look very little like your original idea, but that's okay! I always lead with my purpose of doing what's best for each learner to drive decisions. When you get stuck or feel as if you are spinning your wheels, try the Education Decision-Making Flowchart as a reminder of what matters most.

This chart isn't just for teachers. It's for every person who has a connection to work in education. Use this image to keep the conversation centered on finding solutions for all of our students to become successful in meaningful ways.

What You Should Expect from This Book

Innovate Inside the Box is organized in three parts. Part One focuses on "The Core of Innovative Teaching and Learning." The core comprises aspects of education that are crucial to the success of our schools and students today. My hope is that Part One will refocus your intentions and actions on what will help our students to be successful now and throughout their lives. Below is a visual of the "Core."

Part Two dives into the eight characteristics of the "Innovator's Mindset." Here you will find practical ideas for applying these traits yourself and for developing them in your students. Katie Novak, an expert on Universal Design for Learning (UDL), has co-written these chapters with me and brings a wealth of ideas for making each characteristic come to life in your classroom. Each chapter begins by looking at why each characteristic is essential to our work today in education. From there, we explore how to bring these characteristics to life through the lens of the UDL principles.

The Core of Innovative Teaching and Learning

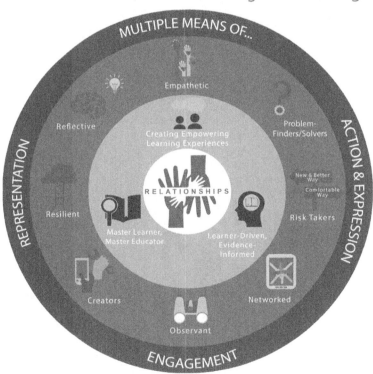

#InnovateInsideTheBox

No single characteristic thrives in isolation, and none of the solutions we provide can be copied and pasted into your work. Instead, use the ideas you find in these chapters to prompt you to find your own innovative solution in your unique context. I often say that the curriculum tells you "what" but not "how." The "how" is what separates great teachers from others and is part of the artistry of teaching. Your teaching can be a work of art if you choose to see it that way.

In the final chapter, we'll wrap things up by asking "What now?" If you are involved in education at any level, you can have a major impact on not only students but also your colleagues. Education is life-changing work! Even as you work to change others' lives, you discover that you are growing and changing as well. In these chapters, I hope you will find the encouragement to take care of yourself so you can serve at your best.

As you read *Innovate Inside the Box*, keep these three questions in mind:

1. What has challenged you?
2. What has been reaffirmed?
3. What will you do moving forward?

My hope is to inspire you to think about these three questions and create your own answers. What you get out of this book will be different from any other educator on this journey, just as it would be for your students. (Side note: As a matter of practice, it's a good idea to have your students answer these questions regarding their experience in schools and in your classroom. Their answers would give more quality evidence of impact than any score from a standardized test could ever measure.)

Moving Forward

As I said in my first book, what I'm sharing in these pages is not meant to be an exact recipe for success. Katie and I can provide ideas and strategies, but you are the one who will bring these ideas to life. Ideas mean nothing unless they are put into action in meaningful ways within our schools.

The teachers who make the greatest difference in the lives of students look beyond the here and now and inspire their students to make the world better than it is. What I want to think about is what would happen if we all embraced the Innovator's Mindset within our schools? What would happen if we used what we knew to figure out what was best for the people we served and to create new and better opportunities for the learners we served? How much better would schools be if our students could share how the majority of adults—or better yet, *all* of the adults they interacted with in their time at school—had a positive impact and inspired them to find their own path? How much better could our students' futures be? Maybe it is crazy to think such a thing is even a possibility, but the fact that you are reading this book indicates to me that you are ready to take action and change the trajectory of your students to not only be better learners but to create a better world.

I am humbled to be on this journey with you. Let's get started.

Questions for Discussion

1. Think of one educator who had an impact on you as a student in a positive way. What did they do that made an impact? I encourage you to reach out to them or share how they made a positive difference in your life.

2. Think of a challenge in your lifetime, be it personal or professional. How did you learn and grow from that experience?

3. What was a constraint you have faced in education and how did you overcome it? What lessons did you learn from that process?

Please share to #InnovateInsideTheBox

PART ONE

The Core of Innovative Teaching and Learning

n Part One of this book, we are going to dive into the elements that comprise the Core of Innovative Teaching and Learning:

- Relationships
- Learner-driven, evidence-informed practice
- Empowering learning experiences
- Educators who serve as master learners

Each one of these elements brings innovative teaching and learning to life. Without them, all the technology in the world won't produce truly successful learners. That's because innovative education isn't all (or even mostly) about a high-tech classroom. I want to be clear from the onset of this book: When I call for innovative teaching and learning, I'm not implying that we need to totally change everything that happens in classrooms and create all-new, digital-dependent opportunities for all students. What I am saying is that we need to create the *best* opportunities for each individual student. In some cases, traditional practices may work great for some learners, while more modern practices may work better for other students. If, for example, your school gives every student access to a mobile device, but you have a student who thrives with the use of pen and paper, don't force that student to go exclusively digital. Whatever individual learners need to succeed is where we begin. Innovative teaching and learning is about creating opportunities that empower all learners—including us—to thrive.

As we explore each core element in the upcoming chapters, my intent is to validate your practices but also challenge your thinking and inspire you to create your own pathway to innovative teaching and learning. Throughout my career, I have worked with many teachers on different types of "evaluation," and, in doing so, I have seen things implemented, such as the Danielson or Marzano Framework, which can be helpful to teachers if they are not seen as prescriptive and punitive. Inspired by teaching frameworks like this myself, I want to share ideas with you, but I want our time together to feel more like a conversation than an evaluation or a prescriptive coaching session.

Here are a few more things to keep in mind as you read Part One:

1. Relationships are in the center because this element is the most important thing in education. Relationships carry more weight than other elements because without them at the center of all we do, all of the other necessary elements are much harder to achieve.

2. I use the term "learners" when discussing anyone involved in education and the term "students" when referring to students. If we do not see ourselves in the word "learners" within the realm of education, we will never be able to bring out the best in ourselves or others who are involved in this profession. Learning, at all levels, is paramount to the work we do in education.

3. While you read this book, I encourage you to reflect both openly and privately, to dig deeper into the information. I have seen many posts on social media encouraging people to read "100 Books in a Year!" Reading is an essential part of being a learner, but from my perspective, it is better to read fewer books, reflect deeply, and create something with the knowledge that you have accumulated than to speed read and change nothing. Please share your learning as you see fit. We all benefit from your ideas. On Twitter or Instagram, use the hashtag #InnovateInsideTheBox to share your thoughts and actions with me and the world. When we see sharing with other educators as part of our work, we elevate the profession as a whole.

4. Look for and listen to others' ideas—especially from those within your current community. The narrative that "you can't be a prophet in your own land" is something that needs to go away in education. This book is meant to spark conversation and to help us all become aware of the teaching professionals around us who have skills and gifts that you or I, or others around the world, don't necessarily have. We live in an amazing time in which we can connect with people around the world, but if we can't connect with people in our local and regional communities, then connecting "globally" will not matter as much. As you read this book, think of both how you can shine your light on the world and, as our profession encourages, how you can encourage others—your colleagues and your students—to shine their lights as well.

Read, reflect, connect, share, and shine. If we all start at the core—relationships—and work our way out from that point, there is no limit to the creative capacity we can unleash in schools around the world.

Chapter 1
RELATIONSHIPS

*I am somebody. I was somebody
when I came. I'll be a better
somebody when I leave.*

–Rita F. Pierson

I was sitting at a table after working with a group of teachers at a conference when a gentleman came up to me and said, "Do you have a moment for a story?"

"Of course!" I replied.

He then placed a rock about the size of my fist on the table and shared a story that reveals the power of our words and beliefs about our students. Here is what he shared:

"Your story about Kyle reminded me of one of my own stories. When I first started teaching, I had a student in my class named Alex who struggled with the work. He had some great skills—skills that I didn't recognize at the time because my concern was more on what he struggled with in my class than how he was talented outside of it. I was there to teach content, not kids.

One day, and I am embarrassed to say this, I was at my wit's end with Alex. I said something that I regret to this day, and it sticks with me. He was struggling with something and I said, 'I could get a rock to learn more than you in this class.' Alex looked at me and said nothing. I continued on with other students and never thought twice about what I said in the moment.

The next day, as I was sitting at my desk, Alex walked up to me and placed this rock on my desk. He looked at me and said, 'F---g prove it,' and walked away. I was destroyed because of what I had done

I have carried this rock in my backpack to school for twenty-five years to remind me that what I do and say to our students can stick with them for a lifetime. I want to find ways to lift them up and never tear them down."

My heart hurts as I think about the fact that there are many stories that students could tell about teachers who have had a negative impact on them. And like the teacher who carried that rock around as a reminder, we all have regrets. We are only human. In one moment, in a single breath, even without realizing it, we can tear down someone's confidence and belief in ways that stick with them for a lifetime.

In the same way, it only takes a few seconds and a positive interaction to be the best part of someone's day. My goal when I was a teacher and a principal was to acknowledge every student and adult I walked past. Whether it is with a simple greeting or kind word, we can each be a bright spot in someone's day.

It doesn't take much to create a positive connection. Josh Stumpenhorst proves that point with a story about a student he said hello to every single day in the hallway in his book *Drawn to Teach*: "At one point in the spring, she shared with me that I was likely the only person who knew her name. I laughed it off and told her that plenty of people surely knew her name. She went on to tell me that she has days where she leaves her house, goes to school, comes home, and the only person to say a word to her was me."

When I first read that story, my heart sank because I know Josh's student isn't the only one who feels so alone. Some of our students are dealing with things that we couldn't even imagine, and a kind word from a teacher, a caring adult who sees them as a person, can mean the world to them.

But it's not only the kind words that show kids we care but our steadfast presence. When we show up every day and we show our students how much we care, we provide a place for them to learn, grow, and be supported. This tweet from Professor Heather Thompson Day is a sober reminder that *erring on the side of positive* is always our best bet for students and adults as well.

Heather Thompson Day
@HeatherTDay

I had a student who was late to class come up to me afterward.

"I'm sorry I was late." He said. "My mom died this morning & I didn't know where to go, so I came here."

& that was the day I decided to treat every single student as if I have no idea what they're going through.

In the brevity of a tweet, Heather reminds us how important our authentic interactions are with every person we encounter in our day and how much these connections matter. In response to this tweet, Wisconsin educator Susan Probst shared in an email with me, how a genuine care and love in our classrooms can make a world of a difference for not only our students, but also ourselves as teachers.

"I worked with an eighth grade teacher once who started every class greeting students at the door with—'I'm so glad you are here.' If the student missed the day before, she would say, 'we missed you yesterday. Class isn't the same without you.' She virtually never had any discipline challenges in her classroom. Parents were amazed at how their child could be in trouble in every other class but not hers. She was sincerely glad that they were there."

David Theriault, an incredibly forward-thinking teacher from California, reminds us that our own paradigm shifts as educators can have a significant impact on the environment our students encounter in our classrooms:

David Theriault
@davidtedu

After 25 years of teaching I've realized that my favorite thing to say, when a student walks in late, is this:

"I'm glad you're here."

We can never truly change others, but as David and Heather embody, our own response to situations can be the catalyst in creating a space where students not only want to be present, but where they want to excel.

Think about your experience at school. What sticks out in your memory? I remember struggling with science as a student. I remember studying all night for the "parts of the microscope" test in my tenth grade Biology class and acing it. When the teacher gave us our marks, I was the only student in the class who had earned 100 percent on the test. I basically felt like Einstein. From that point on (even now), when I've talked with my friends from that grade, no matter what has happened in my life or what comment they make, I often default back to, "But do you remember when I got 100 percent on my 'parts of the microscope' test?" This one success has been my claim to fame! All kidding aside, it is the only test (out of hundreds) that I remember from my time as a student, and even then, I still don't remember all the parts of a microscope. Other than that one test, I don't remember many lessons or projects or tests that inspired me to excel. Only rarely did mastering the content push me to do better.

What I *do* remember are my teachers. They are the ones who encouraged me to do more and try again. And I, too, felt destroyed at times by teachers who showed zero interest in me as a person. It's easy to look back now and see that the classes I struggled most in were the ones where I felt no connection to the teacher or the subject. In those classes, I was a terror. I would rather have been considered a jerk than stupid, so I masked my struggles with academics by going out of my way to be the class clown. Sometimes I wonder how things might have been different for me and for my teachers in those classes if I felt like they actually cared about me—not just my test scores.

I don't want to be too hard on those teachers though, because the reality is that none of us are perfect. It isn't always easy to connect with students. We don't always do it right, but that's okay. Our imperfections and failures are often what make us relatable to our students and the people with whom we work. As my good friend and brilliant educator Meghan Lawson says, "We don't have to be perfect to make a difference. We need to care deeply about our impact on kids, care deeply about our words, and we need to embrace our humanness."

Caring is what is most essential to the work we do every single day. Caring is what enables us to develop relationships with students and colleagues even when it's difficult to find common ground.

Relationships matter in every stage of school, but from my observations, I have noticed that as students move up in grades, connection becomes less of a priority in many schools. Larger classes and busier schedules can make it seem difficult to connect. But even if you are teaching hundreds of students in a semester calendar, each individual still needs to feel important. As one principal shared with me, lack of human connection is often the root of disengagement. By interviewing students who had decided to drop out of school and asking them why, that principal learned that many of the students who quit felt they had no significant relationship with anyone in the building. Caring is what empowers us to connect, and connection is one key to keeping students engaged in their learning journey.

Relationship > Rules

When you are inundated with initiatives and overwhelmed by the pressure and stress that come with being an educator, it can be easy to lose sight of our purpose. But if we stop and ask ourselves, "Why am I involved in education?" the answer will never be "to control my students." Most of the educators I know want to prepare students to succeed in the world we live in, and beyond that they want to empower and equip students to create a better world for all of us to live in. But too often, control, rules, and requirements seem to take precedence over relationships. When that happens, the rules become the primary focus and can negatively impact the way we interact with students.

I do believe boundaries are important; school cannot be a free-for-all environment without falling into chaos. To exist and work well in any space, boundaries are crucial. It's *how* we interact with students and provide them with opportunities to practice social and community skills in school that allows us to develop relationships while enforcing those boundaries.

No one is better at this than *Culturize* author Jimmy Casas. I was blessed to be able to visit Bettendorf High School in Iowa while Jimmy was still serving as principal there. What I loved about Jimmy's interactions with every single person in the school— whether they were a teacher, student, parent, support staff, or any other role—was that he treated each person with value. He addressed each one by name and made every person in that large school feel as if their interaction with him was his most important one in the day. The embodiment of servant leadership, he made sure that each person knew that contributing his or her talents as an individual was crucial to the success of the school as a whole.

While visiting his school, I witnessed two interactions with a student that drove home the value of connection and relationships. At the time, the school had a "no hat" policy. Everyone in the school was aware of the policy, so the student knew he was breaking the rule when a teacher on staff snapped her fingers at him, waved her finger toward his head, and said, "Hat!" Without saying a word, he took off his hat and kept walking. A few seconds later, he looked back to see if the teacher was gone and, with the coast clear, quickly put his hat back on.

About one minute later, Jimmy walked into the hallway and saw the student wearing the hat. He walked right up to the student and addressed him by his first name, which was impressive in a school with around 1,500 students at the time. Being follicly challenged himself, Jimmy started talking about how jealous he was of the student's full head of hair and said that if he had hair like that student's, there is *no way* he would wear a hat and hide it from the world. Jimmy joked around, and even though he never said the words "take off your hat," the student did so with a smile. He put his hat in his backpack and left it there even after Jimmy had left the hallway.

That one interaction between Jimmy and his student was a master class on how to build rapport with students even while enforcing rules. Because he demonstrated care by knowing the student's name and took the time to connect rather than simply lay down the law, the student responded positively. I will be the first to admit that Jimmy's approach took longer, but it was an investment of time that he would get back tenfold.

Small Investments, Big Dividends

Every single day, you have an opportunity to create a space where students and staff members are welcomed and valued. You, like most educators, probably find it easy to stand at the door with enthusiasm and anticipation on the first day of the school year. And like most of us, you probably feel the excitement fade away as the monotony of the day-to-day sets in. That's when it's easy to lose focus on why we got into the profession in the first place. The never-ending to-do list and responsibilities of being an educator can feel draining. I get it. I also know that we have to fight to prioritize relationships with our students and make time to connect, both in and out of the classroom.

It really is the small things we do that matter. When I was a school principal, I made a point to stand outside of the school to greet students and staff members each morning and stand outside to say goodbye at the end of the day. I could often tell by the students' faces if they were having a rough start to their morning. I knew that if I could get them smiling by the time they got to their classroom, the teacher's day would be easier, which, in turn, could make my day easier as well. So I'd tell a joke or high-five the kids as they came through the door. The interactions were simple and brief, but they helped set the tone for the school for the entire day.

Greeting students each morning or hanging out in the hallways or visiting the playground during recess were all part of "supervision," something I once thought of as just one more thing on my to-do list. But when I shifted my thinking to see those times as opportunities to connect with students, each interaction became valuable. As I said earlier, it doesn't take much to create a connection, but it does take intention. Here are a few small ways you can be intentional with the opportunities you have to create connection:

1. **Greet kids at the door.** There is a massive difference between walking into a room and being welcomed and walking into a classroom where the teacher is sitting at his desk prepping for the day. One says, "I'm glad you're here!" The other says, "I'm busy; be quiet." You can set the tone for the entire day by reminding kids that you feel privileged to have them show up each and every day.

2. **Play music as students enter the classroom.** As a sports-lover, this might be something that I am a little biased on. Walking into a room that has lively music playing reminds me of warming up for a game. Music can often bring a smile to people entering the room and is just an awesome way to start the day.

3. **Go out of your way to make your first interactions positive.** At some point, kids make mistakes. As a principal, I would go out of my way to connect with kids *before* they were sent my way for correction. Tough conversations will undoubtedly come, but if a student knows you value them, those discussions will be easier.

4. **Call parents early. Make sure they know you care about their kid.** I learned this awesome tip from a former secretary at my school. It is a fun call to make. Parents are genuinely and pleasantly surprised to hear from their child's teacher when the only reason for the call is a positive one. This is a definite investment in an emotional bank account and lets parents know that you sincerely care about their child.

5. **Plan with flexibility and your students in mind**. What you did last year might not work this year because these are different kids. Don't over-plan; ask questions and learn about your students.

6. **Design the classroom *with* your students**. We spend so much time decorating the classroom before students show up, and then we call it "our room." Something as simple as decorating the classroom together not only gives students ownership of the space but also demonstrates that you care about their opinions. (It can also save you a ton of time!)

7. **Discover and tap into each student's passions**. One of the best ways to work with people is finding out what they love and tapping into it. The teachers who spent time finding out my passions made me feel like they had a genuine interest in who I was and what I loved.

8. **Help students move closer to *their* goals**. We spend a lot of time thinking about where we want students to be and not enough time asking where they want to go. Success is deeply personal, and if we know students' goals and dreams for both in and out of the classroom and help them work towards achieving them, our impact will last long after their time under our care.

9. **Encourage learners to ask questions every single day and then help them find those answers**. As I noted in *The Innovator's Mindset,* if a child leaves school less curious than when she started, we have failed her. Let's ensure that we encourage our students' curiosity. Let's provide lots of opportunities for them to explore and find the answers to the questions they pose and are curious about.

10. **Love them**. This might sound a little fluffy, but teaching is a tough job. So is being a kid. There are so many things that kids deal with while growing up. Sometimes they just need to know that someone cares about them. Go out of your way to show that enthusiasm for your students as people, not just who they are in your gradebook.

What would school look like if these ideas for "student investment" were the norm in education?

Relationships can (and must) be built within the walls of our schools, but the following story from a principal reminds me that little moments we create outside of school can help students feel more comfortable with the adults in the building on a day-to-day basis. Belinda George, a principal in Texas, started a tradition of "Tucked-in Tuesdays," where she would read a bedtime story to her students at 7:30 p.m. every Tuesday evening to keep the "relationship strong between home and school." Many of her students approach her in school because of the time she takes to establish the connections she makes *outside* of the building. She shares perfectly, "If a child feels loved, they will try. There's no science about it."[1]

We do not have to spend every waking hour outside of school finding ways to better ourselves as teachers or connecting with students; personal time away from the profession, especially in a world that is highly connected, is crucial to our all-around well-being. The idea is that when we do interact in meaningful and intentional ways with those we serve, it creates a better environment not only for the student but also for ourselves as professionals. This is an investment of time, not an expenditure, that can pay off in dividends. When those we serve feel valued, they tend to go out of their way to do the same for us.

Connection Isn't Only Important to Students

Now, let's take things a step further in terms of connection. What might happen to the culture of your school if educators (all of us) made these similar investments in one another as colleagues? How might things feel differently if every staff member knew the others' names and maybe their hobbies or the names of their children? The sense of connection would surely improve.

One way we can ensure our colleagues feel valued is to go out of our way to acknowledge them and the amazing contributions they make to our schools. As mentioned earlier, one of my biggest pet peeves in education is the idea that "you can't be a prophet in your own land." Why not? Why do we value the expertise of the educator on the other side of the world more than we do our colleague across the hallway? Teaching is an insanely tough job. You know that because you're *doing* it. The same is true for the person across the hallway, no matter how easy or hard they may seem to make it look. There is *never* harm in positively and authentically acknowledging the contributions the adults in our schools make. Don't wait for someone to leave your building to appreciate them! Say good things about them now, right in front of them! As former NBA player Jalen Rose has said in the past, "People will bring flowers to your funeral but won't bring you soup when you're sick." Don't wait for it to be too late to share a kind message. You will be amazed at how simple, heartfelt words can improve relationships with your peers and change the culture and environment for the entire school.

Students notice the interactions we have with each other as adults and mirror them with their peers. The environment we create for one another as adults is emulated by students, so the environment we want our students to create for one another should be the norm in what we are modeling as adults. Students are always watching; what do you want them to see?

More Than a Warm Feeling

The importance of relationships is not just about creating a warm and fuzzy feeling for our students and staff. It is about creating an environment where learners can excel and bring out the best in everyone around them. As I stated earlier, a simple greeting at the door can make a significant impact on how a student feels and acts that day. A recent study found that when teachers greeted their students positively at the door, academic engagement increased by as much as 20 percentage points, while they saw a decrease of 9 percentage points in disruptive behavior.[2] It's really much bigger than someone's physical presence at a classroom door. It's about positive relationships. Research validates the notion that relationships should be the core of what we do in education, highlighting that a supportive and caring learning environment can positively impact social and academic outcomes, which are critical for success in school, eventually a career, but more importantly, in our own lives. [3,4,5]

Additionally, as the principal I mentioned earlier discovered through interviews with students who had dropped out of school, a lack of relationships can have negative effects on our students. One study found that math competence of students who moved from having positive relationships with teachers at the end of elementary school to less positive relationships with teachers in middle school significantly decreased.[6] This also highlights the importance of structures that allow for educators to build relationships with students and make the time to get to know them. This is why

Students are always watching; what do you want them to see?

many teachers, especially in middle school and high school, have stopped going over the syllabus and diving right into content the first days of school and, instead, now prioritize time spent getting to know students and building community. As both research and practice indicate, that time invested in relationships will be worthwhile in both social and academic outcomes.

How we view relationships can have a tremendous impact on how we organize our days, our learning experiences, and our interactions with students and our colleagues. In the article "Why Relationships—Not Money—Are the Key to Improving Schools," the researchers define "social capital" as the network of relationships between administrators, teachers, parents, and the community that builds trust and the norms promoting academic achievement.[7] Although we often assume that the amount of money spent increases the outcomes, researchers out of Ohio State found the effect of social capital was three times greater than financial investments on math scores and five times larger on reading scores. They highlight that "social capital was not only more important to learning than instructional expenditures but also more important than the schools' poverty, ethnic makeup, or prior achievement." At the core, connecting with people and developing meaningful relationships can help us meet the needs of all students, especially our most vulnerable.

The same study also found that relationships between the adults is equally critical for student success: "Research shows that the more teachers collaborate, the more they work together on instructional improvement, the higher the test scores of their students. That's because collaborative work builds social capital that provides students with access to valuable support." The more we see "relationships" as the core in what we do, whether it is with students or adults, the more likely we will be to create conditions where all learners, not just students, can excel.

Knowing our learners—what drives them, what their strengths are, not only weaknesses—can help them improve academically and, more importantly, become better people. Our focus on relationships is not about being "best friends" with students and/or colleagues. It's about knowing our learners, their strengths, and what brings out the best in each one of them. By getting to know students, we can better understand and co-create learning experiences to suit them individually. We can't continue to discuss the "personalization of learning" (more to come on this in Chapter 2) but only measure our students in standardized ways.

In *The Innovator's Mindset*, I asked the following question to help educators calibrate their thinking to the experiences within their learning environments: *Would you want to be a learner in your own classroom?* Often when I pose this question, it pushes people to reflect on the experience for learners in their own classrooms. And in many cases, teachers with whom I have discussed this question say they would love to be in their classroom because they see the experience as one from which they would benefit. That's great; however, what worked for the teacher isn't necessarily what works for all students. This question is meant to encourage seeing the learning experience from the viewpoint of the students you serve currently, which means knowing the students in front of you is crucial to your collective success.

When we measure "success" in schools, it is often through the lens of academics and grades, but a school, I would argue, should provide much more than that to our students. I definitely benefited from academics as a student in school, but I also learned a significant amount about leadership from playing sports, about creativity from my fine arts opportunities, and about interacting with people from conversations with peers and faculty in the hallways. Principal Brad Gustafson puts it this way in his book, *Reclaiming Our Calling*: "Teaching the whole learner doesn't mean we disregard academic achievement; it just means we refuse to disregard everything else important."[8]

Schools have to be about more than academics. Some of the most creative and innovative students in your school may struggle in standardized metrics and structures of school. If we only measure their intelligence and abilities by how well they do on a test, we will never inspire them to find their own path to success, as they define it for themselves today and in the future. Getting to know and honoring each one of the learners we serve in our schools is a pathway to bring out the best in each individual within our community.

Moving Forward

Rita F. Pierson, in one of my favorite TED Talks of all time, shared the following statement: "Kids don't learn from people they don't like."[9] I love the statement, but I have seen it challenged often by people who ask, "Isn't it possible to learn from people you don't like?" Of course it is. Every person reading this right now has learned something from a person they disliked or a situation that was negative. We can find opportunities for learning in any situation if we are willing to look for them.

Rita's statement, however, points to the truth that we can learn *so much more* from those with whom we have a positive connection. Relationships don't serve only to build up our learners; they give us a foundation to be able to challenge them as well. And the truth is, we are more likely to rise to high expectations when they are held by someone we like and trust.

If schools do not push our students to grow, then there is no purpose for them to be there in the first place. But if there is no relationship where learners feel seen and cared about, when we push our students or colleagues, there will be little motivation, if any, to respond to that encouragement. How do you find that balance between building up and challenging others to grow? Ask yourself these questions:

1. Do I have any positive connection other than this initial interaction, and do they know their contributions are valued?

2. Do I ever connect with this person to say something positive, or do I only share feedback with others (or specific people) when it is negative?

3. Am I open to being challenged and critiqued in the same manner in which I am ready to deliver?

The common denominator in all three questions is the importance of the reciprocated relationship. Ultimately, you can learn without a relationship, but you will also go much further when one is present. Knowing and being known are not everything in education, but with positive relationships, our ability to effectively teach, inspire, and empower our students to make the world a better place today and tomorrow increase exponentially.

Questions for Discussion

1. How do you build relationships and know your students as individuals inside and outside of your classroom?

2. Think of two or three teachers who influenced you as a student, either positively or negatively. How has that made an impact on you today?

3. Share a story on social media (blog or video) about a time that you saw an impact of "relationships" as a learner or teacher.

Please share to #InnovateInsideTheBox

Chapter 2
LEARNER-DRIVEN, EVIDENCE-INFORMED

I am different, not less.

–Temple Grandin

*D*ata-driven **is the stupidest term in education.**

If you've heard me speak at a conference or school or district meeting, you may have heard me use that phrase before. I say it often when working with educators because I know it's a sure way to get the audience's attention.

If I am speaking to a group comprising mainly teachers, that statement is usually greeted with applause (after they look at their administrators to see *their* response). If I am in a room full of administrators, the response is often shock and concerned looks. Both groups sincerely want to do what is right for their students, but when I say that "*data-driven* is the stupidest term in education," what each hears can be very different. With either type of crowd, my hope is that the jolting statement helps us all recalibrate our focus and reminds us of our true purpose in education: opening doors for those we serve. After all, no one who ever dreamed of being a teacher did so imagining just how *meaningful and exciting it would be to test kids*! (I hope you can hear the sarcasm in that last sentence!)

When I denounce the term *data-driven*, the first challenge that comes in response is usually, "Are you saying *data* is not important?"

Not at all; in fact, this whole chapter is focused on the importance of ~~data~~ evidence and how it is crucial to serving students. *But we should be driven by students, not data.*

I struggle with the word *data* in education because of the disconnect between what it actually means and how the education system tends to wield it.

Here is the Merriam-Webster definition of data:

> *factual information (such as measurements or statistics) used as a basis for reasoning, discussion, or calculation.*

Here is what many teachers hear or feel when the word is used: *letters and numbers.*

> **But we should be driven by students, not data.**

As shared in *The Innovator's Mindset*, when we are data-driven, we take the most human profession, teaching, and reduce it to simply letters and numbers. There is something inherently wrong with this approach because when teachers are driven by test scores, the students themselves get lost in the process.

Talking about summative and formative assessment moves the conversation in a slightly better direction, but what if we shifted our focus and our practice to be *learner-driven* and *evidence-informed*? With relationships at the core of what we do and learner-driven, evidence-informed practices, education improves dramatically for teachers, administrators, and, most importantly, for students.

Why Use the Word *Evidence* over *Data*?

The words *evidence* and *data* have similar definitions, but the way they are often perceived in the world of education is significantly different. Evidence seems to encompass much more than letters and numbers. It helps us not only look for things that can be measured but also things that *can't* be measured, things that have an impact on students' learning experiences. Evidence can include tests or assignments. It also includes ideas and thinking shared in portfolios, self-assessments, interactions in the hallways, concerts, sporting events, fine arts performances, internships and exhibits, and anything else that highlights and demonstrates learning and growth. We fail to tell the whole story of a learner when we focus on a narrow view of success in education in the all-mighty pursuit of scores.

Elements of education that are not solely academic receive less attention because they are harder to record and measure, but does that make them less valuable? No; in fact, I would argue that the things that are difficult to quantify are at least as valuable to our students' long-term success as any grade they will ever receive. Attention to both social-emotional and academic

> **We fail to tell the whole story of a learner when we focus on a narrow view of success in education in the all-mighty pursuit of scores.**

25

skills acknowledges that we are multifaceted beings. My ability to write this book, for example, is due in large part to literacy skills I learned in school. Those skills were easily assessed by tests. But the way I tell a story or give a presentation has a direct connection to the opportunities I had to participate in drama and fine arts as a student, where the things I learned were far more subjective in nature. My point is that focusing on learner-driven, evidence-informed practices does not mean we forgo either "academic" or "non-academic" learning; it means that *all* of these experiences are important to our students' success.

For those who cling to tradition and scream, "But the real world *demands* grades!" I have to ask: Does it? Really? Maybe that was true in an earlier era. Maybe. But that certainly isn't the case today. In the 2013 *CNET* article, "Google: GPAs are worthless" (Want to guess where this article is going based on the title?), Laszlo Bock, former senior vice president of People Operations at Google, said, "GPAs are worthless as a criteria for hiring, and test scores are worthless." He went on to say, "Google famously used to ask everyone for a transcript and GPAs and test scores, but we don't anymore, unless you're just a few years out of school. We found that they don't predict anything."

Here's what the company is doing instead:

> Google is now tending toward something called "behavioral interviewing." This seems to involve actually wondering what you're really like and how you really live, think, and act.
>
> Explained Bock: "The interesting thing about the behavioral interview is that when you ask somebody to speak to their own experience, and you drill into that, you get two kinds of information. One is you get to see how they actually interacted in a real-world situation, and the valuable 'meta' information you get

about the candidate is a sense of what they consider to be difficult."

. . . Google now knows what it really needs. Said Bock: "You want people who like figuring out stuff where there is no obvious answer."[1]

Many of the skills that organizations are asking for go beyond what academics can provide. If you look at the "2022 Skills Outlook" provided by the World Economic Forum, many of the skills that are growing in importance are extremely hard to label with a grade.

2022 Skill Outlook	
Growing	**Declining**
• Analytic thinking and innovation • Active learning and learning strategies • Creativity, originality and initiative • Technology design and programming • Critical thinking and analysis • Complex problem-solving • Leadership and social influence • Emotional Intelligence • Reasoning, problem solving and ideation • System analysis and evaluation	• Manual dexterity, endurance and precision • Memory, verbal, auditory and spatial abilities • Management of financial, material resources • Technology installation and maintenance • Reading, writing, math and active listening • Management of personnel • Quality control and safety awareness • Coordination and time management • Visual, auditory and speech abilities • Technology use, monitoring and control

If you are reading this book, it is very likely that you are involved in education. Think about your first job at a school: How much do you believe your high school or college transcripts played a part in whether you received that job? As a principal who hired teachers and support staff, GPAs never factored into my decision. I was often surprised by the fact that many excellent educators did poorly in school. These teachers, in particular, seemed to "get" the students who struggle because they *were* those kids. I also learned that a high GPA didn't guarantee that candidate would make a great teacher. I can almost guarantee that you have encountered a teacher who did well in school as a student (academically) but struggled to teach. So many factors beyond academic achievement have an impact on a person's ability to teach students. In the same way, grades cannot be the final measure of our students' potential or success.

My good friend Michelle Baldwin, a teacher and administrator at Anastasis Academy, recently reminded me how little, immeasurable things can be hugely important for some of our students. During a visit to her school, a young student who was maybe six or seven years old walked up to me as I entered the classroom, extended her hand, and welcomed me into the room. It was a really sweet moment, and I was extremely impressed by the student's kindness and welcoming nature. We chatted for a bit as she shared what she was learning. When Michelle and I left the classroom, her sense of pride about the encounter with this young student was obvious. Michelle told me that the student I'd met had dealt with a lot of anxiety about meeting new people. One of the goals she had set up for herself, with the help of her teacher, was to improve her ability to interact with new people. Because this young learner knew she was in a safe space with a nurturing educator, she stepped outside of her comfort zone to welcome a new person to the classroom.

Now imagine giving that student a grade on our interaction. Michelle didn't need a grade to see evidence of growth. The evidence was right there in the interaction. But had the girl received a grade on her handshake, her ability to have a conversation, or her level of kindness, the reality is she might be deterred from even trying. Data and grades, with their finality and stigma, are different from evidence and feedback. Feedback is crucial for learning and growth, but grades can actually deter and stagnate learning. My blog is meant to be a space to share evidence of *my* learning. I appreciate and welcome comments from educators around the world. Their feedback helps to expand my thinking. But I know that if someone started grading my posts, I would be less likely to want to continue.

What Is the Evidence of Success?

An article in *The Chicago Tribune* titled "Student petition says too much pressure to succeed at Naperville North" discusses the academic pressure students feel. The poorly worded title insinuates that the students don't want to be successful, which is not the truth. The students are not against success; they are against success being measured in a way that is solely determined by others.

Is that not a fair request? What you consider successful could be wildly different than how I define success. Do we really believe that there is only one answer to what defines success? Or do we as individuals have some say in how we define, measure, and experience success?

Here is a snippet from the article:

> *"At Naperville North there is one path to success," the petition said. "This path is made clear from the day high school anticipation begins, and is reiterated until graduation. From the age of thirteen, every prospective Naperville North student understands that this path makes no exceptions, and those who wander*

off or fall behind are left for failure. Everyone here understands that there is no worse fate than failure.

The petition calls on administrators to 'start defining success as any path that leads to a happy and healthy life. Start teaching us to make our own paths, and start guiding us along the way'"[2]

I do not know enough about this school district to criticize its educators or administrators, and I certainly know there is always more to a story than any article presents. (Being an administrator for several years, I understand how a community or media can share their perspectives freely, while a school isn't always capable of sharing its perspective because of privacy and ethical concerns.) That being said, kudos to the students for sharing their voices. And kudos to the district for doing some very focused work on social and emotional learning.

Allowing learners a greater say in defining success is not about being soft on the students. Personally, I expect anyone who is working toward success to put in the time and effort and often, when people are invested in their own goals, they go above and beyond goals that we set for them. I love the Simon Sinek quote, "Working hard for something we don't care about is called stress. Working hard for something we love is called passion."[3] Learner-driven practice is not about having low expectations; it is about ensuring that the students have a voice in

> # Working hard for something we don't care about is called stress. Working hard for something we love is called passion.
>
> —Simon Sinek

setting those expectations in the first place. School should open doors for students, and not just the ones we (the adults) want them to go through.

Success means different things to different people, but reread this quote from the student petition: *"Start defining success as any path that leads to a happy and healthy life. Start teaching us to make our own paths, and start guiding us along the way."* Again, kudos to them for sharing their voice, understanding that the opportunities provided for them in school today will have an impact on their lives long into the their future—*their* being the important word in the last sentence. How can we do better in schools to help students to create their own paths that lead to happy and healthy lives?

Many educators, even those who agree that the definition of success can be different for everyone, can't seem to let go of grades, saying, "But we still have standardized tests, and grades are important for their future!" Grades might be important, but if you recall the skills that were shared above from the World Economic Forum, skills like innovation and critical thinking, creativity, and learning to learn are the top skills that industry is looking for. Doing well on a test or getting a 4.0 isn't the end goal.

I'm about to say something that those educators, and maybe even you, won't like. The goal of education is not to ensure that every student goes to a post-secondary institution. Isn't our goal to help *open doors* for our students to be successful in their lives in ways that are meaningful for them today and tomorrow?

I am not saying that you should completely ignore student grades. That would be an easy thing to write in a book, but if you put that sentiment into practice, you could lose your job because you'd be ignoring the constraints of the system you work within. Also, grades *are* important for some students, depending on their career choice, as they are still a factor for getting into post-secondary schools. That's why I talk about opening doors.

We must create opportunities for all students to succeed, and we do that, at least in part, by ensuring that we are not closing the door to opportunities for our students. Although many adults feel that a quick Google search gives them the knowledge and understanding of a medical doctor, having that information is not enough to obtain a job as a doctor in a hospital. Or, an example a little closer to home, having "attended school" doesn't give a person the qualifications to become a teacher. You have to go to a post-secondary institution for both of those careers. Our job is to make sure we do whatever is necessary to ensure students have access to learn about and pursue career paths that align with their strengths, interests, and values.

The beauty of our world is that we all bring different gifts to the table. So why do schools tirelessly and intentionally (or unintentionally) try to equip our students with all the same skills and knowledge? We have to acknowledge that our students come to us with a unique mix of experiences, strengths, weaknesses, and passions. What we want for our students may not be what they want for themselves. In my generation, students were told over and over again that university was the only road to success; not going was considered a failure. But we have to stop thinking of "smart" as only "doing well in school." I have had plumbers come work at my house, who likely did not go through the same "formal" education that I did at the post-secondary level. But when they were at my house working, their brilliance was on full display in doing things that I simply did not understand. Our calling or task is to expose students to numerous pathways and provide them with the skills to be self-directed and goal-oriented so they can choose or create a path that allows *their* brilliance to shine.

If we really want students to guide their own path and lead happy and healthy lives, this will require us to define success differently. Rather than approach students with a deficit mentality, we must look for and build on their unique strengths and talents and help them acquire the skills, knowledge, and mindsets they need to see themselves as full of possibility. That's how we will help them find their place in the world and achieve their definition of success. That success starts now, and it isn't all about a grade on a test.

School Is About More Than a Future of Work

As our youth see people their age doing amazing things, either because of or in spite of school, their perception of what is possible and important expands. That's one reason I encourage people to quit saying, "We are developing the leaders of tomorrow." Those words imply that students can't make a difference until they are out of school, which is simply not true. Beyond that, my belief is that school has a bigger purpose than preparing kids for a life of "work."

Educator Dean Shareski shares in his post, "Stop Following Your Passions . . . the Celebration of Work," that who we become because of school is as important, if not more so, than what we eventually do:

> *The shift I've made of late in terms of talking to my own kids is not to suggest they don't pursue their passions but do not necessarily tie their passions to their vocation. It's great if you're able to go to work at something you really love, but that doesn't have to be the case. My daughter is an artist but has decided that she doesn't want to make a living as one. For many reasons, including the idea that mixing work with your passion often takes the joy out of it, she's chosen to teach. She seems to be enjoying that but certainly views it much more as "work" than a passion. I think that's okay.*

I have many friends who have regular "jobs" like accountants, railroaders, and engineers. If they won the lottery tomorrow, they would quit those jobs. That's not sad; that's the reality. Part of the reason you might feel sad is because of the way we've demeaned work as something to be avoided. In a culture devoted to "me" and "self-esteem," it seems incongruent to spend eight hours a day doing something you don't really love. Many think you should only do work you really love. How selfish is that? People work for many reasons, and working to support a family, survive, make a contribution to your world is not demeaning. The more we as educators and parents tell kids how important it is to find their passion and tie that to their vocation, the more we are telling the bus driver, the janitor, the waitress, and the gas station clerk that they are failures. The problem with our schools remains that they are largely designed to train students for university, to get "good" jobs.

A few years ago, I attended a career education conference and heard career counselor Kristin Cummings say, "Stop asking kids what they want to be and start asking them, 'How do you want to live?'"[4]

That great advice reminds us that grades will mean very little long-term in the entirety of our lives. Rather than seeking a "good" job or following the prescribed path, what if, in contrast, we helped students find purpose and develop skills and mindsets that can have a lifelong impact?

Do Students See a Larger Purpose in Their Learning?

In Canada, many of our schools teach French. In my view, there are two ways you can teach the language. You can focus on every student getting an "A" (the more data-driven way) by covering the material, testing, reteaching, and documenting what was retained with a test. Or you can do something that is much more challenging and more meaningful: teach students to become "fluent" (the learner-driven, evidence-informed way). Teaching for fluency is tough. You have to know the kids in front of you, and they have to see value in and deeply understand why the content is important. Knowing the students allows you to understand what drives them, so you can tap into it and help them develop the intrinsic motivation to eventually learn on their own. This approach rarely aligns with a pacing guide or scripted curriculum, as learners will move at different paces and take various paths. But the payoff of teaching for fluency goes far beyond the grade. Here's the deal: If you can help students become fluent, getting the A will probably be easy. But I can also tell you that as a student I often received an A in my French class, but I can speak very little French today. I did what I had to do and got out of the class as soon as possible. My focus was solely on obtaining a result rather than purposeful learning, so the results were temporary.

Katie Martin, author of *Learner-Centered Innovation*, created the graphic below to show the difference between performance orientation questions (which focus on grades) and learning orientation questions (which focus on depth of learning).[5] Understanding the difference can help you identify, through students' questions, whether they see a deep value of the learning that is happening or if they see the work as just part of a "checklist" to complete.

WHAT QUESTIONS ARE LEARNERS ASKING?

Performance Orientation Questions

- How many pages is this supposed to be?
- Did I do this right?
- What do I have to do for an A?
- Is there extra credit?

Learning Orientation Questions

- How can I make this better?
- Did I accurately communicate my ideas?
- Is there another way to solve this problem?
- What is the impact that my work has on others?

My high school experience in French mirrors what is happening in far too many classrooms across various subjects today, where the focus is on a performance orientation. Even if the students earn an A, that "success" doesn't carry with them into life.

To make learning last, the point can't be to simply regurgitate content; learning must be about teaching students to think, problem-solve, and communicate. For that to happen, we must help students develop a learning orientation so they can see a deeper meaning to what they are learning and, more importantly, the skills necessary as they continue to learn within their school experience and take it with them wherever they choose to go. And *that* kind of learning requires innovative, learner-driven, evidence-informed teaching. (Are you seeing a theme?)

Revealing Purpose through Innovative Teaching and Learning

In speaking with educators around the world, I know most teachers *want* school to have a bigger purpose for themselves and their students. It is the reality of grades, tests, scores, and curriculum that seem to stand in the way of meaningful learning. But those barriers are also not going away any time soon, which is why it is crucial to "innovate inside the box."

Have you ever asked your students, "What do you want to do when you get older?" and received the answer, "Be a YouTuber"? (If you haven't, just wait!) Let's be honest; many adults laugh when they hear students say they want to be a YouTuber, but why? Do we expect our students to want the same jobs we wanted at their age? Or do we want our students to take advantage of the opportunities they have in front of them today? You know the right answer here. Remember, our goal is to open doors. And even if the career of YouTuber feels far-fetched to you, it isn't a completely unrealistic expectation for your students. At the very least, learning to communicate through video is a powerful skill that is already being used in countless careers around the globe.

If you doubt that there are job opportunities in the video medium, let me share just one example. "Ryan's Toy Review" is a YouTube show during which a seven-year-old plays with and reviews toys on his channel. He was the top YouTube earner in 2018 at an estimated $22 million for the year. That figure doesn't include the earnings from his toy line at Walmart or from his show on Nickelodeon.[6,7] Again, the point is not to focus solely on money, but if students have the opportunity to share something they are passionate about and make a living from it, isn't this an opportunity we should want to create for them or, at a minimum, equip them to explore?

So let's say you have a student who wants to be a "YouTuber," but you have to teach the science curriculum. Consider having the student create a YouTube video that explains the objective. Not only will you tap into this student's passion *while* teaching the curriculum, you will provide the child an opportunity to share her learning with the world—and in creating an opportunity for the student to share her learning, you level up the learning experience another few notches. At a recent conference, Rushton Hurley explained why sharing their learning with a wider audience—like the YouTube universe—matters: "When students do it for the teacher, they want it to be 'good enough,' but when they do it for the world, they want it to be 'good.'" An authentic audience makes the learning relevant and gives purpose to what students create.

Many people will say, "This idea of tapping into students' strengths and passions is great in theory, but we still have to teach the curriculum." Well, the video example I provided teaches the curriculum while going above and beyond. The curriculum is a "minimum" requirement; it is okay to go above and beyond. But teaching the curriculum while tapping into the strengths and passions of the student is using their abilities to "do your job" while bringing out the best in those you serve. *How you teach the curriculum* is *the innovation.*

> # How you teach the curriculum *is* the innovation.

I want to share one more low-tech example of innovative teaching that leads to greater learning. It comes from a guest post titled "Delaying the Grade" by Kristy Louden on Jennifer Gonzales' must-read site for educators, *The Cult of Pedagogy.* Kristy shares how, even when working within a system that still expects "grades" for our students, getting students to focus on learning, not just grades, can have a much bigger impact on student learning and growth in the long run:

> *The solution was remarkably easy and accidentally originated out of my laziness (score one for being a little lazy!). Last year, kids had turned in essays on Google Classroom, but rather than pasting a*

completed rubric into their essay as I usually did, I made hard copies of the rubric and wrote on them. This meant that I could return papers with comments but without grades.

And from this a whole new system was born: Return papers to students with only feedback. Delay the delivery of the actual grade so student focus moves from the grade to the feedback.

*The simple act of **delaying the grade** meant that students had to think about their writing. They had to read their own writing—after a few weeks away from it—and digest my comments, which allowed them to better recognize what they did well or not so well. The response from students was extremely positive; they understood the benefit of rereading their essays and paying attention to feedback. One boy said, "Mrs. Louden, you're a genius. I've never read what a teacher writes on my essay before, and now I have to."*[8]

Kristy's strategy recognizes that "grades" are a reality in our system but can actually deter from deep learning (more on that in a few paragraphs) while providing feedback for growth is crucial for development. When we think differently about how we "innovate inside the box," deep learning and grades can coexist.

Kristy's strategy is learner-driven and pulls evidence from students while working within a system and *eventually* assigning a grade. It's a great reminder that the solutions to most of the problems in education can be answered from within the system rather than by it. If you're waiting for someone else to change the system, you might be waiting forever. Look for ways to make changes within the system that help your students thrive.

What We Nurture Is What We Grow

You've heard the statement, "The grass is always greener on the other side." The version of this sentiment that I like best comes from Neil Barringham, a community inclusion advocate from Brisbane, Australia: "The grass is greener where you water it." (I won't lie; I first heard this quote from Justin Bieber's song "As Long as You Love Me," which is why I know it. But Neil gets the official credit!)

What part of our students do we nurture?

Some educators describe their school's process of "Response to Intervention" as one that focuses solely on where students struggle. From there, they seek to provide different levels of support to help the students develop through these supports. In simpler (and harsher) words, the system focuses on what the students are terrible at and how they (the students) could be "fixed." With all the attention turned on the students' weaknesses, no effort is made to proactively eliminate barriers to learning. Nor are their strengths nurtured.

I know this is a very simplified and generalized explanation for a complicated issue, and is not the norm for all schools, but this process of focusing on what people *can't* do, however gentle or harsh, happens too often in too many classrooms. And it does more damage than good. The intention, of course, is to help students, but the impact likely has the opposite effect.

Let's apply this process to educators and consider the outcomes. Let's say I am your principal, and I sit down with you and identify all your weaknesses. I then figure out ways that I can "fix" you. Day in and day out, my focus is on reminding you of your failings and trying to fix you. How long would you want to work for me? I don't think many teachers would want to be in that environment and fewer still could thrive there. Why would our students be any different?

This is not to say that we shouldn't help develop the weaknesses of our students, but our focus should be on their strengths. Let's start there. When people feel valued, they are more likely to show up and tune in physically and mentally. That's when they have the best chance to learn and grow. As Temple Grandin, a professor at Colorado State University and autism spokesperson, says, "There needs to be a lot more emphasis on what a child can do instead of what he cannot do."

A strengths-focused approach to education isn't about fluffy ideals meant to shield our students from criticisms. The article "The Clifton StrengthsFinder; Can Focusing on Strengths Really Make a Difference?" points to research showing that focusing on one's strengths can lead to higher levels of purpose:

> *In the 1950s, psychologist Donald O. Clifton asked the question, "What will happen when we think about what is right with people rather than fixating on what is wrong with them?"*
>
> *Here are some of the results they found:*
>
> - *People who use their strengths are 3 times as likely to report having an excellent quality of life.*
>
> - *People who use their strengths are 6 times as likely to be engaged in their jobs.*
>
> - *People who learn to use their strengths every day have 7.8% greater productivity at work.*[9]

Although these studies are focused on "work-life," the ideas can easily be applied to the classroom. When they focused on finding "strengths," these are the characteristics they found from employees:

- *Team members look forward to going to work.*
- *They have more positive than negative interactions with co-workers.*
- *These team members treat customers better.*
- *They will tell their friends they work for a great company.*
- *Daily, they will achieve more.*
- *Team members focused on strengths have more positive, creative, and innovative moments.*

I know school and work are not the same thing, but there is a lot we can learn from the world of work that we can apply to our school context. Simply replace "team members" with the word learners (meaning *everyone* who is in an education community), and switch some of the words in the sentences above and see how this would fit our school community. Take a look:

- Learners look forward to going to school.
- They have more positive than negative interactions with peers.
- These learners treat each other better.
- They will tell their friends they are part of a great school.
- Daily, they will achieve more.
- Educators and students that focus on strengths have more positive, creative, and innovative moments.

If focusing on a strengths-first approach helps create the outcomes listed above in classrooms or schools, it would be much easier to develop weaknesses as well. Being "learner-driven," and knowing our students and ensuring they feel valued, is part of creating an environment where they can flourish. As inspirational speaker Alexander Den Heijer notes, "When a flower doesn't bloom, you fix the environment in which it grows, not the flower."[10]

5 Questions to Reveal Your Students' Strengths and Interests

Although there are many tools out there that you could use to help identify what drives our students, I think sometimes the best approach is to ask them directly. A straight line is often the quickest path. With that in mind, here are five questions to ask students at the beginning of the year.

1. What are the qualities you look for in a teacher?

We are quick to share our expectations for our students, but how often do we give them the opportunity to share their expectations of us? If students have been in school for a few years, the teachers they have connected with the most have obviously had some impact. I am not saying you should change your entire personality to suit each child, but I think understanding the characteristics that have helped your students connect with their teachers may help you more quickly develop strong relationships with them.

2. What are you passionate about?

Knowing what a student is passionate about not only helps you bridge connections to their learning, but it also helps you bridge connections to them as human beings.

Years ago, my school held an "Identity Day" (led by our awesome assistant principal at the time, Cheryl Johnson), where all students and staff shared one thing that they were passionate about in a walkaround display. Through this event, teachers discovered ways to connect their curriculum to what piqued the interest of the students, which made it much more relevant to them. Sharing what they were passionate about also empowered the students and helped create new connections within the school community.

3. What is one BIG question you have for this year?

Jamie Casap, chief educational evangelist at Google, Inc., says, "Don't ask kids what they want to be when they grow up. Ask them what problem they want to solve." Whether you tie this question to your course or not is entirely up to you, but giving students the opportunity to stoke their own problem-finding and problem-solving abilities in your classroom will simultaneously empower your students.

Will Richardson, in his article, "Curiosity is the Cat," says that curiosity should be the "Fifth C" and is probably the most important aspect of twenty-first-century learning:

> *Think of most skills, all the stuff that doesn't show up on the report card, all the stuff that probably matters more than the stuff that shows up on the report card, and you'll find they are steeped in curiosity. Problem-solving, problem-finding, persistence, cooperation, adaptability, initiative . . . Which of those doesn't require being curious first and foremost? Can you be any of that if you're not?*[11]

People who change the world for the better are often the most curious. The ones who are constantly asking questions. The ones who are always wondering, "What if?" Great ideas often start with asking questions, not with answers.

Don't just ask this question at the beginning of the year. Check in with your students about their big question periodically. Have they found the answer? Has the question changed? And ask how you can support them. Empower students to be the leaders of today, not only tomorrow.

4. What are your strengths and how can we utilize them?

If you are challenging your students (as you should be), at some point you will find their weaknesses. But remember, we aren't going to start there. Start by asking about and valuing their gifts, talents, and strengths. Research shows that focusing on strengths leads to more confidence, more creativity, and happier lives (amongst other things).[12] By focusing first on strength, when weaknesses do show up, you and your students (and staff) can address them from a place of genuine relationship with an eye toward improvement, rather than seeing them as flaws that need to be fixed.

5. What does success at the end of the year look like to you?

The hard thing about this question is that students will often say what they believe the adults want to hear. Consider adding something like "beyond your grades" (no student wants to do poorly academically in your class or curriculum, whether they are interested in the subject or not), which might help them think about achievements that will last with them past their time at school.

We all define success differently, so find out what their important measures are for this year. Once students have clearly identified what success means to them, work with them to achieve it. In doing so, you can help build important habits that go beyond school.

Many learners (including adults) tend to identify successes through the eyes of others and often compare themselves. This practice is not helpful and can lead to feelings of inadequacy. If we decide our own measures of success and feel comfortable learning from the successes of others, it puts us on a constant path of growth, while learning to focus with "the end in mind." This is an important skill at any age and is one to start early with our students.

Think of these "Five Questions" (listed in short form for reference below) and how you can modify them in age-appropriate ways for your students. How would knowing the answers to these questions for our students, both from the educator perspective and the student perspective, help shape a much more positive experience in our classrooms?

5 Questions to Ask Your Students To Start the School year

What are the qualities that you look for in a teacher?

What are you passionate about?

What is one BIG question you have for this year?

What are your strengths and how can we utilize them?

What does success at the end of the year look like to you?

Moving Forward

How we assess drives our teaching, not the other way around. Being "learner-driven" doesn't mean we toss out measurable goals; it means that we focus on purpose-filled learning that has the potential to impact students' lives well *beyond* the classroom. Being "evidence-informed" does not mean that we ignore academics or the system we work within. Instead, it forces us to figure out ways to help learners grow their strengths so they become better students and better people.

With a learner-driven, evidence-informed practice, we still set goals; the difference is that those goals are relevant to our learners' success now and in *their* future. In my own journey to become healthier, both mentally and physically, for example, I set a goal to run at least 100 miles each month in 2019. The "100 miles" is one of my targets to help me get to a larger goal of becoming healthier, so I can have more energy when I spend time with my family, feel healthier when I travel, and perhaps become a senior Instagram model one day (kidding ... kind of). My measurable goal is part of a larger picture. I track my progress using the Aaptiv exercise app (which I highly recommend). I can also see and feel a difference in my health and energy level.

Too often the grade is the goal for our students, and we lose sight of learning in pursuit of a number. School needs to be something bigger than a grade. Our focus must be preparing students to be successful now and in their future in ways that are meaningful to them. The most important research we can do as educators will always be to know the learners we serve. That's how we ensure all doors are wide open for those we serve to find success on their own journey.

> **The most important research we can do as educators will always be to know the learners we serve.**

Questions for Discussion

1. What might a wider definition of success be for your students or your community? How can you get your students involved in defining success for themselves in short- and long-term planning?

2. What evidence can be used to inform student goals and progress beyond standardized test scores? Share with others how you use this evidence to create better learning opportunities for your students.

3. How do you leverage the strengths of the learners you serve in your classroom, school, or organization?

Please share to #InnovateInsideTheBox

Chapter 3
CREATING EMPOWERED LEARNING EXPERIENCES

The test of a good teacher is not how many questions he can ask his pupils that they will answer readily, but how many questions he inspires them to ask him which he finds hard to answer.

–Alice Wellington Rollins

In 2018, I had the pleasure of hearing Maanasa Mendu and several other students share about their innovative projects—projects that they had been inspired by their teachers to explore. Maanasa, a freshman at the time, was helping to kick off a meeting with a passionate group of educators in Mason, Ohio (near Columbus). I make a point to talk to students and get their perspective as often as I can, but what I heard from Maanasa blew me away! At thirteen years old, she had created a five-dollar, clean-energy device. After I heard her speak, I found this article from the area's *Journal-News*:

While visiting India, Mason High School freshman Maanasa Mendu saw many people without electricity and knew she wanted to make a difference.

"Our family often visits India in the summer. If you've ever been there, the summers are scorching, and they always have these power cuts," she said. "I was like, 'Why don't they have instant access to the electricity grid? What if you could create an off-grid solution to this problem?'" So Mendu decided to be a part of the solution and designed an affordable device capable of generating clean energy. Her innovation recently earned her a spot as a member of the Forbes 30 Under 30 Class of 2017.[1]

She did this at thirteen years old! I was lucky if I finished math homework assignments (odd numbers only, because the even number questions had the answers in the back) at that age. But this young lady is already making a difference in the everyday lives of human beings around the world.

The article explains Maanasa's thinking behind her five-dollar device:

"Over 1.2 billion people in the world lack access to electricity. And for those of us who do have access to electricity, 93 percent of it comes from non-renewable resources that are both harmful to the environment and are also depleting," she said. "Only 7 percent of it comes from renewable sources of energy. . . . The reason why we are unable to apply renewable sources of energy in such a widespread application is due to some of its limitations."

Initially, her project focused on creating a wind energy harvesting device applicable in urban areas and at low wind speeds by using piezoelectricity, or the electric charge that accumulates in certain materials caused by applied mechanical stress. "I wanted to help mitigate the global energy crisis by creating a device utilizing piezoelectricity materials that are both eco-friendly and cost-efficient," Mendu said. "I decided to utilize this by applying the vibrations of low wind speeds and just general ambient environmental energy around us and create electricity in that form."

Please don't ask me to explain any of what Maanasa just shared. Seriously. I have no idea what she did or how she did it, but what I can tell you is that she is having a significant impact on the world.

When educators or politicians say things like, "We are developing the leaders of tomorrow," what students often hear is, "You have to wait until you are out of school to make a difference." Maanasa's story proves that students can make an impact *right now*. Maanasa and the others who spoke at the meeting that day had been inspired and empowered by their teachers to seek out a problem they wanted to solve and ideas they wanted to explore. Others, as media outlets like to remind us, achieve great things not because of school but in spite of it. Because you are reading this, I know that you, like me, want to be part of the reason students succeed. That means we have to create empowering learning experiences for our students—opportunities to learn, question, innovate, and share their ideas. And for *all* of our students to thrive today *and* in the future, it also means that these kinds of experiences and opportunities need to be the norm, rather than the exception.

Why Does Empowering Our Students Matter?

You have probably heard or read that "50 percent of the jobs that will exist in five years don't exist today." My first thought when I see bold statements like this is, *How does anyone actually know this?* When I was a kid, I asked my Magic 8 Ball to predict the future and got answers like, "It is decidedly so," or "You may rely on it." I just asked the Magic 8 Ball about the jobs of the future and got an answer that's probably a bit more accurate than that 50 percent claim: "Cannot predict now." The truth is, we can't know exactly how many new kinds of jobs will exist in five, ten, even fifteen years. What we do know is that the marketplace is changing more quickly now than ever before.

Thomas Friedman notes in his book *Thank You for Being Late: An Optimist's Guide to Thriving in the Age of Accelerations* that this pace of change presents numerous challenges to us as a society:

> *Indeed, there is a mismatch between the change in the pace of change and our ability to develop the learning systems, training systems, management systems, social safety nets, and government regulations that would enable citizens to get the most out of these accelerations and cushion their worst impacts.*[2]

No matter how you look at it, change is happening quickly. Those changes demand that we work with our students so they *do not need us* to learn. If we are going to enable them to thrive in this changing world, *empowering* them to develop the skills and motivation to solve meaningful problems is more important than ever. As my friend, educator, and author, A.J. Juliani states in his co-authored book, *Empower*, "Our job is not to prepare students for something. Our job is to help students to prepare *themselves* for anything."[3] We don't know what the future will predict, but we need to ensure that we help our students develop the mindsets to not only deal with change but also to create something with the change that comes their way.

Empowerment > Engagement > Compliance

I've long believed that change isn't to be feared; it is an opportunity to do something amazing. Choosing to view change in a positive way makes all the difference between feeling terrified or thrilled. As learners, we can look at change in two ways:

1. Change *will* come our way. We can "go" through it or "grow" through it. We grow when we seek out solutions rather than letting obstacles hinder us.

2. We can initiate change; in fact, the most important and meaningful changes are often the ones we choose to make.

Whether we initiate it or not, change is inevitable. It always has been. Change is also a key reason that creating empowering learning experiences is one of the essential elements of innovative teaching. By empowering our students, we help them develop the skills to create their own solutions when they face change.

You may have noticed that *engagement* isn't part of the core. That isn't because engagement is no longer important. It is. But if students are empowered, they will definitely be engaged; the reverse isn't always true. Let me explain: Engagement is often about what you can do for your students. Empowerment is about helping students figure out what they can do for themselves. Empowerment takes learning to the next level.

For decades, the school system has operated with a focus on compliance. Many have shifted to engagement. This is definitely an improvement in terms of creating a more meaningful learning experience, but what today's learner needs is more opportunities for empowerment. This is not to say that "compliance" is obsolete

> # Engagement is more about what you can do for your students. Empowerment is about helping students figure out what they can do for themselves.

in education. It is a necessity to some degree in our world today. The IRS probably wouldn't appreciate if I decided to file my taxes in a really compelling PowerPoint presentation. I have to follow the instructions to the letter or face consequences. Compliance is a skill to develop, but it should not be the end goal or purpose of the work we do in education.

This simple table shows the connection and levels between compliance, engagement, and empowerment, and how each relates to the use of Twitter by educators for professional learning.

As indicated by the statements in the "Empowered" row of this chart, empowerment is not only about the opportunities learners create for themselves but also about the importance of "purpose" in the learning.

When we consider what *engagement* looks like in our classrooms, we may envision students doing the following:

- *Listening*
- *Reading*
- *Observing*
- *Consuming*

The action changes, however, when we envision what *empowerment* looks like:

- *Speaking*
- *Writing*
- *Interacting*
- *Creating*

CEE	Quick Definition Statements	What it looks like	The Simon Sinek Scale (Why?)	Example statements related to the use of Twitter in Professional Learning
Compliant	Learning because I have to.	Have little to no interest in learning material but doing as I am asked to do.	Seeing the "how" but not understanding relevance for learning.	"Why are we doing this?"
Engaged	Learning because I am interested.	Have an interest in what is being shared and can see relevance.	Starting to see "why" from someone else's perspective and seeing relevance to learning.	"This is actually pretty cool. I never thought of using it that way."
Empowered	Learning because I want to and see value in creating a difference for myself and/ or others.	Creating, making, and connecting learning that is meaningful to the individual. Learning is becoming intrinsically valuable.	Starting to create their own "why" and connecting to real life, eventually creating something of value.	"I started connecting and learning with others through #kinderchat. It has really changed the way I do things in my classroom."

As you can see, engagement is crucial to empowerment in learning, not separate from it.

*You will be better at **speaking** if you are good at **listening**.*

*Your **writing** will probably benefit from **reading** the work of others.*

Ultimately, empowerment is about ownership and agency. Providing opportunities for voice and choice in learning is how we create learning experiences that empower learners. Students are more likely to develop as lifelong readers, for example, if they are empowered to choose books based on their interests, as opposed to being limited to only books at "their level."[4] I would have had more interest in reading as an adult (it took me until my thirties to start reading for joy) if, as a student, my reading material wasn't only assigned based on my teachers' decisions. I was always interested in reading *Sports Illustrated* but was told that "magazines weren't real reading" and were not appropriate material for school time. That conversation repeats in schools across North America today, but instead of magazines it's blogs and graphic novels that are labeled as unworthy of school time. Yes, part of our job as passionate educators is to expose students to great books, materials, and other opportunities that encourage students to learn things they perhaps wouldn't access on their own. The point is to remember to allow for ample choice. Reading, like everything else in our lessons, should empower our students to drive their learning.

Asking Better Questions

So how can you empower students when you feel stuck with a certain curriculum? One simple way to "innovate inside the box" is as simple as shifting your (and your learners') focus from getting the right answers to asking better questions.

In *A More Beautiful Question*, Warren Berger discusses how asking great questions is essential for growth and progress in not only the learner but society as a whole:

> *On some level, we must know—as the business executive knows, as the school teacher knows—that questions are important and that we should be paying more attention to them, especially the meaningful ones. The great thinkers have been telling us this since*

the time of Socrates. The poets have waxed on the subject: E. E. Cummings, from whom I borrowed this book's title, wrote, "Always the beautiful answer / who asks a more beautiful question." Artists from Picasso to Chuck Close have spoken of questioning inspirational power.

. . . Scientists, meanwhile, have been great proponents of questioning, with Einstein among the most vocal champions. He was asking smart questions from age four (when he wondered why the compass pointed north), and throughout his life Einstein saw curiosity as something "holy." Though he wondered about a great many things, Einstein was deliberate in choosing which questions to tackle: In one of his more well-traveled quotes—which he may or may not have actually said—he reckoned that if he had an hour to solve a problem and his life depended on it, he'd spend the first fifty-five minutes making sure he was answering the right question.[5]

A while back, I posed this question on Twitter: How can we teach the curriculum but still develop problem-finders within our system? (Note: We will discuss problem-finders more in-depth in Chapter 6.) Wendy Johnson replied with an incredible example of how a little shift in thinking can make a huge difference in our classrooms:

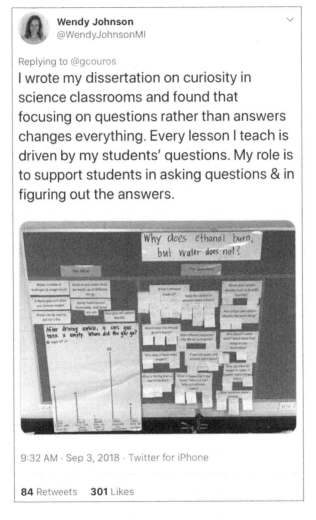

Even if students are not terribly interested in the content being taught, when they are asked to figure out great questions and explore solutions, as opposed to memorizing and regurgitating answers (as Wendy suggests in her tweet), they will experience more profound learning and develop mindsets that will serve them beyond their time in the classroom. Giving them the opportunity to brainstorm questions helps them develop the essential learning skills of inquiry and embodying curiosity.

In her book, *The Power of Why: Simple Questions that Lead to Success*, Amanda Lang discusses the importance of curiosity and its connection to intelligence:

> *Curiosity is, therefore, strongly correlated with intelligence. For instance, one longitudinal study of 1,795 kids measured intelligence and curiosity when they were three years old, and then again eight years later. Researchers found that kids who had been equally intelligent at age three were, at eleven, no longer equal. The ones who'd been more curious at three were now also more intelligent, which isn't terribly surprising when you consider how curiosity drives the acquisition of knowledge. The more interested and alert and empowered you are to seek answers to your questions, the more you're likely to learn and retain. In fact, highly curious kids scored a full twelve points higher on IQ tests than less curious kids did.[6]*

Curiosity, Lang explains, also empowers students to develop the ability to learn how to learn, which in our dynamic and constantly changing world is the greatest skill that a learner can acquire. Rather than simply having students memorize information that may be irrelevant in years to come, we can empower students by providing opportunities to learn how to think and to develop skills that will help them face new challenges and solve new problems. If we can inspire wonder in children, they are not only likely to become successful in school but also more likely to find meaningful ways to make an impact on the world *because* of their experience.

The Importance of Students Leading Their Own Learning

Dr. Erin Lawson, an educator from St. Louis, Missouri, realized as she was sitting in classrooms judging presentations that students lacked presentation skills and that there wasn't actually an opportunity for them to gain those skills. As a result, she sent a survey to the entire high school student body asking them one simple question: "If you could come to school to learn about anything you wanted, what would that be?" Within an hour, she had received 150 responses. In an email, Erin shared with me that the students' *desire* to learn prompted her to create an experience that made a powerful impact with the students in her school and is now being implemented in schools across her state:

> *In March 2016, we had the first Student Personal Development day for high school students. How to change a tire, cook simple meals, create YouTube videos, buy a car, prepare for college, etc., were a few of the many sessions that our students voiced they needed. They even got to register for sessions so the entire Student PD day was personalized for their wants and needs. Flash forward to 2019: schools around Missouri have implemented their own #StudentPD event with success.*

When students have opportunities to share their questions, like the one created by Erin, they are more likely to view learning as something that is valuable—because *they* feel valued. When they have the chance to voice their choice, the journey and the destination of learning become far more meaningful to them. Although we want to create experiences like this as a "norm" in schools, even one-off days like this can help educators see what is possible in their classrooms and how empowerment positively affects the learning and motivation of their students.

Providing empowering learning experiences also increases students' willingness to endure some of the mundane or "compliant" tasks of education. Think of it this way: When you work for someone who doesn't care about you as a person, every task seems pointless. The opposite feeling exists, however, when you feel as if you are part of a larger purpose. Even the boring or tedious tasks of school (and life) are made bearable when we feel that we have at least some measure of control. As I mentioned earlier, compliance will always exist in facets of school and life, but when the ultimate focus of education is empowerment, we can do great things within the constraints of school.

What about the Basics?

As I push educators at all levels to focus intentionally on innovation in schools, I often feel a counter push of "back-to-basics" thinking. If you feel a similar concern for the basics rising up in you, let me clarify something: Being an innovative school or teacher doesn't mean you abandon the "basics," it means you are focused on going much further than what *only* teaching the basics could provide. It means that you look to the learners and create new and better experiences that empower students to meet the desired learning objectives and develop skills to be successful now and in their future.

Innovative educators ensure that students learn to write, but rather than assigning the standard five-paragraph essay that feels pointless and will only be read by one person, these teachers look for opportunities to meet their learning objectives in ways that are meaningful to students, such as writing books, blogs, video scripts, and so much more. Students can't do any of those things without developing and practicing the fundamental skills of reading and writing. When students are empowered to choose how they can best demonstrate their knowledge and skills, they are able to see the relevance in learning the basics and how reading, writing, and math apply to their lives and are less likely to check out mentally.

This is not to say that "old methods" are better or worse than newer ones. The point is that our focus must always be on depth of learning. William Chamberlain left a comment on my blog related to these thoughts. He said, "We can't create deeper learning or connections between what we know and what we need/want to know without that background knowledge already being in place. A simple example would be you cannot orally communicate very well if you never learned to speak."[7]

I agree with William. The larger point is that the ability to read doesn't matter much if we don't understand what we are reading, or we no longer want to read. Yong Zhao summarizes this beautifully: "Reading and writing should be the floor, not the ceiling."[8]

Clearly, the basics are important; it's how we go about helping students acquire the skills they need to succeed that matters. If our students leave school with a solid grasp of the basics but hate *learning*, we have done them a disservice. Simply knowing the facts isn't enough.

I might better be able to retain facts shared on a topic, but it doesn't mean I understand them or can do anything with the information. Remember that parts of the microscope test I talked about in the introduction? Even though I correctly labeled each part back in tenth grade, I would not be able to pass that same test today. That information was retained for the test, then forgotten as soon as that class was over. That's why when I work with educators, I challenge people to create something with the information I have shared, whether it is by writing a blog post, drawing an image of information, sketching a reflection, recording a podcast, creating a video, or using any other type of media. If we really want to process, interpret, analyze, or reflect on what we have shared, we will need to make our own connections, not simply rely on the connections that others make for us. If we *understand* information on a deeper level and do something with it, we also are more likely to *retain* it as well.

When you see research that debunks a "new method" in favor of an older one, ask whether the findings are focused on "deep learning" or on "doing school" well. Katie Martin, author of *Learner-Centered Innovation*, makes an excellent point on this very notion: "If the world is changing, the evidence and research become irrelevant if you don't consider a new context."[9]

If schools focus simply on "retention and regurgitation" of information, we are less likely to influence the Maanasa Mendus of the world. The "basics" are a start and essential, but are definitely not an endpoint.

The Process of Innovative Teaching and Learning

Less us, more them.

–Gary Stager

Innovation is not about a *product* as much as it is about a *process* or way of looking for problems and solutions. Think of it this way: Every "best practice" in education was at one time an innovation. Someone, or some team, saw a need in their classrooms or schools and created a different idea or pathway to fill that need or to address what wasn't working. Nothing that has ever been deemed "best practice," however, works best for all students done in the exact same manner. Not. One. Thing. If there was one thing that worked for every child in the world, everyone in education would know what it was and would be using it in the exact same way all of the time, and all of our students would be thriving.

As an example, formative assessment is a high-yield strategy for learning, but to be most effective for each student, great teachers will make iterations on how it is delivered.

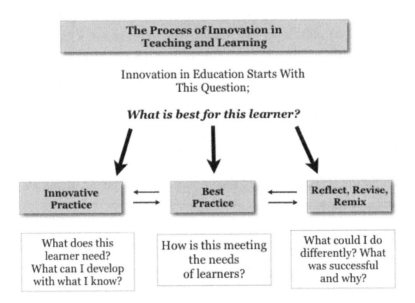

The Process of Innovation in Teaching and Learning

Innovation in Education Starts With This Question;

What is best for this learner?

Innovative Practice	Best Practice	Reflect, Revise, Remix
What does this learner need? What can I develop with what I know?	How is this meeting the needs of learners?	What could I do differently? What was successful and why?

The best educators find a balance between using what they know, remixing what they know, or creating something entirely different, to serve the students in front of them. The "best practice" is to constantly be asking, "What is best for this student?" and then creating learning opportunities that meet the specific need. It is essential to understand that there is never a "standardized solution" to serve students who have individual needs, strengths, skills, and experiences.

In *The Innovator's Mindset*, I shared this, and it's worth repeating here as we think about the reason for creating empowered learning experiences:

> *Inspiration is one of the chief needs of today's students.*
> *Kids walk into schools full of wonder and questions,*
> *yet we often ask them to hold their questions for later,*

so we can "get through" the curriculum. We forget that our responsibility isn't solely to teach memorization or the mechanics of a task but to spark a curiosity that empowers students to learn on their own.

To wonder.

To explore.

To become leaders.[10]

The focus on *creating empowered learning experiences* is not only about helping our students create a better future for themselves, but also to develop opportunities that get them excited about their own growth and development in schools today. To do that, these empowered learning experiences should be something we, as educators, create *with* our students *for* our schools and classrooms. And like so many innovations in our school, these experiences are often the result of discovering a need or problem and allowing students to become part of the solution.

One example of this comes from a time early in my career when I served as the "tech integration coordinator" for my school. Many of my colleagues thought that meant I had the ability and time to fix anything that conducted electricity. Being on call to fix technology was a part of my "job" that I hated, but still did my best to fulfill. One day, out of sheer frustration, I sent one of my students to help a teacher get a device up and running. The student was so excited, he asked if he could help out more. And that's when our student IT department launched! From then on, students helped teachers with technology issues. They loved being able to use their skills in a way that actually helped people and, because they knew there was a good chance they would be called upon to fix something if it broke, these students took ownership of the technology in the school. This innovative, empowering solution of a student-led IT department was a win-win for everyone involved.

Daneen Baller, a high school business teacher with Willoughby South High School in Ohio, shared the following story with me about an endeavor she started to give students the opportunity to experience the reality of running an actual business within school. By offering a real-world opportunity, she created an empowering learning experience that ensures her students develop and retain relevant skills and knowledge.

> As a teacher of Business Education, I had the idea that students could learn to run a business by starting and running a school bookstore. I was reading The Innovator's Mindset at the time, and I tossed the idea out to my principal with some generalizations behind it. He was very supportive and encouraged me to develop the concept further. The more I read, the more I became determined to make this a reality. The store would contain spirit wear, school supply items, required novels to read for class, and general spirit items. I envisioned a mini-college bookstore for our high school.
>
> In my class today, students learn business concepts and apply them to the school store. They make all the decisions: what to buy, how much to order, what price to charge, when to have sales, how to track inventory, create a financial forecast, advertise, and make sales pitches to generate business. They set goals and are so focused on meeting them. They give up their lunch periods to run the store. They volunteer to work in the evenings when we have open house or a basketball game. They don't even care that they aren't getting paid.

A tough lesson for them to grasp was that we couldn't just buy whatever we wanted and put it in the store. We had to make sure that we had money in the account to buy it. We had to learn to budget our money and still earn a profit. Another difficult lesson was when they spent money on an item they were sure would sell, and it didn't. They had to learn how important it is to do market research. They've learned soft skills, such as problem-solving, communication, teamwork, and leadership. It's been such a pleasant surprise to watch students step up as leaders.

Students can now take the class for two years. The first year, they learn the basics. In the second year, they learn the management piece.

We like to say we built the airplane as we were flying it. It was messy, I had serious doubts about what I had gotten myself into, but the energy and excitement the students had most days was undeniable. They loved this class. They wanted to be successful. They wanted to represent their school, and they had a lot of pride in doing so. This idea and vision has become a reality.

This experience has changed me as an educator. I feel like I threw the rule book out the window and have made more of an impact on my students in the past two years than I did in the first twelve.

Daneen's story reminded me of two things. First of all, it is more important to provide *real* opportunities for learning, not only *relevant* opportunities. To the person who says, "School should prepare students for the real world," this is a great story to remind them that schools are preparing students for the real world by placing them in *real-world* situations. The skills learned through this process are things that I did not learn in high school, but that would have helped me tremendously. Secondly, Daneen reminded me that the lessons students will remember when they leave school are the ones that create a sense of purpose.

The Impact of Leadership and Ownership

Both of the previous stories mentioned both ownership and leadership. These are, in fact, essential to empowering learning experiences. Beyond the intended lesson, this sense of personal pride that students feel when we empower them to own their learning impacts the classroom in other ways. Over and over again, I've seen how empowering students can shift classroom management to classroom leadership and ownership. Teachers often tell me they have noticed that the more they focused on empowering their students, the less work and classroom management they had to deal with. As students take ownership of the classroom, the net result is that they are much more interested in the learning. When you are considering where and how to create empowered learning experiences *with* your students, ask the question A.J. Juliani and John Spencer pose in their book, *Empower*: "What are you doing for your students that they can be doing for themselves?"[11] Use that as a starting point to take the learning in your classroom to new heights.

Moving Forward

Early in my career, an opening-day speaker said, "Why is it that educators walk out of school at the end of the day so tired, and kids have so much energy? Shouldn't it be the opposite?" That always stuck with me, and the more I thought about it, the more I focused on empowering students. Eventually, I came up with three simple questions to develop student ownership of their learning:

1. What will I learn?
2. What will I solve?
3. What will I create?

If you choose to work with your students to answer these three questions, you would be amazed at all they could initiate in their lives *because* of school. My recommendation is that you allow these questions to be your GPS for learning—something you and your students constantly revisit and use to recalibrate and redirect the journey of learning and growth.

I've found that documenting the answers to these three questions (as well as the process of discovery) provides evidence of learning by showing growth over time. Documentation can be done through audio, video, writing, or whatever format the student feels comfortable with, but there would definitely be a benefit in both the application and reflections being accessible to more than simply the teacher.

Questions like these are meant to help our students shine, not to dim their light by forcing them to use methods that don't work best *for them*. I believe the point of education shouldn't be conformity; it should be to ensure that students develop a love for learning as well as the skills to learn and thrive. Empowering them to *not* need us is the best way to ensure they are successful on their path. It also benefits us, as educators, as we tap into the most powerful (and often underutilized) resource in our schools: our students.

If you want to prepare effective leaders of the future, there is no better time than today to give them those opportunities to impact the world. The ultimate hope for empowering our students, after all, is that they will shine their light on the world—now and throughout their lives.

Questions for Discussion

1. If we look at what students are doing in the classroom as a sign of the effectiveness of their teacher, what are some examples of things you would look for from students to signify great learning?

2. What are some examples of "empowering learning" in your classrooms for students and in your school/organization as professionals? How are you empowered as an educator, and how does that empower students in learning?

3. Curiosity and questioning are keys to empowered learning. What are some ways you can help students develop powerful questions to spark their curiosity?

Please share to #InnovateInsideTheBox

Chapter 4
MASTER LEARNER, MASTER EDUCATOR

A teacher can never truly teach unless he is still learning himself. A lamp can never light another lamp unless it continues to burn its own flame. The teacher who has come to the end of his subject, who has no living traffic with his knowledge but merely repeats his lesson to his students, can only load their minds, he cannot quicken them.

–Rabindranath Tagore

I f you believe, as I do, that growth is essential to the work we do in education, there are probably at least a few moments you look back on in your career with some sense of embarrassment. You can likely point to a few lessons (or years) and honestly say, "I would never do it like that now. I've come so far. I can't believe I ever did that!" The same will be true ten years, five years, or maybe even one month down the road. You'll look back and see how you've changed and how your practice has improved. In a profession where learning is the focus of our job, growth is essential and the target is always moving.

Just to be clear, I am not writing this book as *the* master learner. I know there will always be more to learn. I *am* a voracious learner, particularly when it comes to education. My wonder, curiosity, and openness to ideas, both new and old, have served me well, and, I hope, have benefitted those with whom I've worked through the years. My parents get the credit for instilling and nurturing those characteristics in me.

My parents, who were both immigrants to Canada from Greece, have modeled learning for me in so many ways. Both with limited education (Mom's formal education ended with grade six, and my father with grade two), they not only handled change, but thrived in it. They did so much to create opportunities for my three siblings and me through their willingness to adapt, take risks, and try new things. My mom, now in her eighties, is extremely comfortable with technology. Yes, her Facebook account is quite the wild card; I never know what she is going to post next. And if you put a mobile device in her hands, she will start pressing buttons until she gets it to do what she wants. Her fearlessness regarding technology reminds me of the narrative that kids are better with technology than adults is false; kids, unlike so many adults, just haven't lost their willingness to push buttons.

And when you consider that the iPhone is designed to be so easy to use that anyone can open the box, start pressing the (very few) buttons, and make things happen, there's no reason *not* to push buttons! My mom

> The narrative that kids are better with technology than adults is false; kids, unlike so many adults, just haven't lost their willingness to push buttons.

learned quickly that all she had to do to call her relatives in Greece was to ask Siri to Facetime them. Compared to making an international call on a rotary phone, which could take a good sixty seconds if there were too many nines in the number, getting Siri to connect her is a snap!

My dad's impact on me today even after his passing, not only as a father but as a learner, has shaped a lot of what I do today. The experiences he had throughout his life are hard for me to imagine having to handle. He lost a sibling at a young age, fought in a war, and moved across the world not knowing if he would see his family again. These things shaped him in both positive and negative ways. My dad rarely showed affection to me as a young child, but our last words to each other before he passed away in 2013 were "I love you." Those three words were rarely spoken by my father until I was in my twenties. I don't fault him; he grew up in a different time. Knowing what I do about him now, I can understand why he wasn't always a warm man, and I can see how showing emotion was something he had to learn how to do.

My mom shared a story with me about a simple encounter the day my father passed away that showed his true nature. She had taken him a soda to go with his lunch that day, and as she handed it to him, he looked at her and said "thank you" in a way that my mom had never seen before. I know it seems like a little thing, but my mom felt love and kindness in those words in a way she had not felt consistently from my dad. He was a grateful person but definitely had trouble showing it. But not in that moment. After lunch, my father went to take a nap. He died peacefully in his sleep that afternoon. His sudden death was not something my family expected (although maybe he did), and this story reminded me of how my dad showed that even until his last minutes, he was willing to grow. Mom sees that "thank you" as all-encompassing, as if my father was thanking her for everything she had done for him in his life. I like to think that's true. Even in his last moments, Dad was learning. In this case, it was learning how to effectively show the gratitude he felt. This has shaped a lot of how I think today.

For my parents, learning—a new language, new job skills, new technology, new communication behaviors—helped them succeed despite incredible challenges. Learning holds that same kind of importance for all of us, but there are instances as educators when we think, *I'm good*, and choose to dismiss new ideas or evidence without much consideration. Whether the information we reject is based on in-depth research or anecdotal evidence from peers, it feels easier to simply continue doing what we have always done.

Willingness to learn is not age-related; it's about mindset. No matter how young or seasoned you are, if you are open to growing as an educator, you will look for learning everywhere—whether it is in an education book, a commercial you see that connects to something you do in the classroom, a conversation with students' parents, a movie, or anything else you do or see in life. That's what it means to be a master learner. And if you want to grow as a teacher, learning will become a way of life.

We know learning and growth are important, but how often do you see people fight change in education? How many times have you felt that resistance yourself? I get it. Change rarely feels comfortable or easy. If you break down what it really means to fight change, however, in many instances, what we are actually fighting is learning and growth. I am not saying all change is good or that all "old things" are bad. What I am saying is that when we are averse to even considering how change may lead to something better for our students (which, in turn, leads to something better for ourselves), perhaps we are in the wrong profession.

I'm not sure I would have been so direct with that last statement were it not for the self-awareness of a principal I talked with a while back. He was attending a professional development seminar that I was leading, and as we talked privately, he shared that he was really struggling with some of these "new ideas" I had shared in the session. He was extremely gracious and complimentary of what I was doing, and I learned a ton from him that day. A few weeks later, a friend sent an email regarding a speech this principal had given at his retirement banquet. In the speech, he shared that after our talk at that meeting, he had decided that it was time to retire. He loved the ideas I was sharing and understood how quickly things were changing in education, and he decided that he no longer wanted to keep up. He was extremely proud of his career, and explained that he wanted to retire on a high note rather than staying on for the sake of staying. He implored the educators in the audience that night to commit to continual learning. And, he said, if someone wasn't willing to do that, it was time to move on from the profession.

At first, I felt horrible. My initial worry was that I had sent a good educator into retirement. Stepping back, I know that isn't the case and that it's far more likely that any mention of me was just part of a good anecdote for a retirement speech. His powerful message, however, will stick with me forever. I hope I never grow tired of learning, but if I do, I hope that I have the courage to leave the profession before I stand in the way of anyone else's learning and growth.

The Difference between *Learning* and *Knowing*

You know quite a lot. Your experience and education have helped you acquire all sorts of knowledge, and that's a very good thing. The knowledge you bring to your school community each day benefits your students and your colleagues and helps inform your practice. No matter how much you know, however, you will always need to be learning.

Knowing is static. *Learning*, in contrast, is active. I *know* the date of my birthday. That will never change. But I am learning how to adjust to things as I get older. I can know a certain practice has worked for students I have worked with in the past, but that is no guarantee they will work for students today or in the future, because there is always this changing variable: the students in front of me.

Both knowledge and the ability to learn are vital to our success, whatever our role in education; for example, if you teach a certain subject area, your knowledge of that content area is crucial. But like a jazz musician who knows the basic notes on the scale and the mechanics of playing the saxophone, the ability to improvise depends on the other instruments in the band, the musicians he's playing with, and what song that they are playing at the time. Improvising—adjusting to all those factors—requires him to learn even as he plays. Likewise, *learning* is your ability to use your own depth of knowledge to then improvise in order to serve the students in front of you.

Research is an important element for learning and growth and often informs ideas and practices to try in education. Yet, for some reason, a persistent belief in education exists that innovation and research are opposites. Based on that, some people resist innovation, believing that *all* practice should be informed by vetted research. That attitude totally discounts the wisdom and the experience of teachers in the classroom! Yes, we should use any relevant research to inform our practice, but we must also be willing to adjust as necessary for the benefit of our students. Frederick M. Hess summarizes my thoughts on this topic succinctly:

> *Research should inform education policy and practice, but it shouldn't dictate it. Common sense, practical experience, personal relationships, and old-fashioned wisdom have a crucial role to play in*

determining when and how research can be usefully applied. The researchers who play the most constructive roles are those who understand and embrace that messy truth.[1]

As stated in Chapter 2, we have to acknowledge that research often focuses on "what improves scores" and not necessarily on "what improves learning." We have to understand that distinction. Will Richardson, in his post "On Learning . . . In School,"[2] suggests that we are asking kids to learn things in school that they haven't chosen or maybe even don't care about. Then we measure learning using "very narrow, quantitative indicators" to determine how well a child does in school when, in reality, those indicators may not be valid measurements at all.

We should regularly ask the question, "Is this focused on test scores or deep learning?" Even as we work within the constraints of a system driven by scores, we should never sacrifice the latter for the former. If we decide that schools should be a place for deep learning (for all of us) and acknowledge the constraints of scores, I believe we can learn and find solutions that allow both to be achieved. (We'll get into the strategies and solutions in Part Two.)

Three Types of Learning That are Crucial for Educators

Being a master learner requires that we look at learning in three ways: learning *about* our students, learning *for* our students, and learning *from* our students.

Learning *about* Our Students

Who are the students in front of you? What are their stories? What are their strengths and what gets them excited to show up to school each day? Remember that the core of innovative teaching and learning is relationships. If we don't understand the learners we serve, even the best ideas for teaching and learning will not be as effective if we don't learn about our students and connect with them first.

The misperception I had when I first started teaching overlooked the importance of putting relationships first. I believed that the *best* teachers were those who came in two weeks early to photocopy everything they would need for the entire year. They *knew* that by the fifth Tuesday of school at 10:12 a.m., their students would be at a certain point in math, no matter what it took to get them there. I aspired to have those organizational skills and to have a plan that would work out flawlessly. As I grew older and more experienced, I realized I had misplaced my priorities. The teachers whom I had admired for their precision planned to teach content, not their students. They planned everything without ever even meeting them. What I learned from experience, as my carefully organized plans fell short, was that I needed to adapt to my students and their needs rather than expecting them to adapt to my teaching. When I did that, I was able to maximize our opportunities for learning.

In his article, "The First 6 Weeks: Strategies For Getting To Know Your Students," Mike Anderson explains why and how knowing our students on a personal level can positively impact the entire classroom:

> *First, the better we know our students, and the more they know we know them, the more invested they become in school. Also, a dynamic and vigorous learning environment is built on relationships. When we create strong connections with our students, we create a learning environment where risk-taking and collaborative learning can take place.*
>
> *Finally, the better we know our students, the better we can help craft learning experiences that match who*

they are. Knowing our students is fundamental to real differentiation.[3]

The issue of dividing one's time amongst so many students, especially at higher grade levels, is an undeniable challenge, but that doesn't mean we don't try to connect with our students daily. As a high school teacher, I would spend lunches playing basketball or guitar with students, so I wouldn't just get to know them, but they would know me as well. When I spent time doing things I enjoyed with students—things that were not solely focused on academics—the relationships that grew as a result made my time in the classroom easier and, honestly, more rewarding. I focused on learning their names and getting to know their interests, which helped me better see how to tap into their strengths. I wish I could say that I got to know every single high school student in my class at the same deep level I felt with the students in my elementary school classes, but I would be lying to you. That being said, I knew many more students because of these actions I took than I would have if I hadn't even tried. I know that these kids made an impact on me and, hopefully, I made an impact on them.

Building time in our day to connect with students who may be struggling can make an impact not only on that student but also on the entirety of our classrooms. In the ASCD article "Assuming Our Best," Rick Smith and Mary Lambert share the "Two-by-Ten" strategy and the impact personal connections have on the classroom.

Raymond Wlodkowski did extensive observations of student behavior, cataloging student time in and out of seat as well as the types, instances, and severity of student disruptions. In particular, he researched a strategy called "Two-by-Ten." Here, teachers focus on their most difficult student. For two minutes each day, ten days in a row, teachers have a personal conversation with the student about anything the student is interested in, as long as the conversation is G-rated. Wlodkowski found an 85 percent improvement in that one student's behavior. In addition, he found that the behavior of all the other students in the class improved.

This can be counterintuitive. But the students who seemingly deserve the most punitive consequences we can muster are actually the ones who most need a positive personal connection with their teacher. When they act out, they are letting us know that they are seeking a positive connection with an adult authority figure and that they need that connection first, before they can focus on learning content.[4]

Learning about our students is more than discovering how they learn; it's about creating personal connections and understanding *who* they are. Every child in our schools needs to feel that their teachers care about them as an individual—not just a score. The goal of learning about our students, as with all of education, is to help them go and grow further because of us, not in spite of us.

Learning *for* Our Students

It may seem obvious to say that learning is important. Learning is a norm in how we perceive the work that we do in education to become better for our students. What I have noticed, however, is that too often we get so focused on jumping into the "teaching" aspect of our work that we skip the "learning" portion for ourselves entirely. Here are just a couple examples. See if you recognize the tendency to skip learning: We want to implement digital portfolios with our students, but do we first create digital portfolios for ourselves so that we can understand what the learning can look like and what opportunities it will open for our students? If we are teaching our students to write, are we writing in different mediums to understand the potential and limitations?

This book has been greatly aided by my own digital portfolio curated in my blog, which is online and accessible to anyone in the world. Some of the ideas I am sharing right now came from ideas I've shared in my portfolio. In truth, my portfolio is more like a library I have curated with my ideas and the valuable ideas of the people who inspire and educate me. Having my own digital portfolio has taught me its value. And here's how that carries over to students and their learning: Say, for example, I am teaching probability in fifth grade and ask students to find a video, under five minutes, that explains certain elements of probability. Instead of me doing the work of finding resources, analyzing whether they are beneficial, and then showing the video to students, the students are tasked with doing this work for themselves. (Sometimes the work we do for our students actually takes away incredible learning opportunities from our students.) Now the students have found a video, analyzed it in their portfolio, and then shown a deep understanding of the concept based on their work. Imagine moving ahead two years to see those same students in seventh grade. When the concept of probability comes up, they are not solely dependent on their memory because they have created their own library of learning that they can access to help them with concepts they learned in earlier grades.

Had I not first gone through the learning process of creating my own digital portfolio, I could not have given you this example. My learning informs my teaching, and the same is true for you. If you want to be a master educator, you need to be a master learner. This means we have to understand what

> **If you want to be a master educator, you need to be a master learner.**

learning opportunities exist now, and in the future, to leverage for the benefit of our students. As Katie Martin states so well in *Learner-Centered Innovation*, "If we want to change how students learn, we must change how educators learn."

Once again, the "time" question arises, and rightfully so. As an administrator, I was adamant about giving teachers time during their professional learning days to play with new technology and figure out how new concepts could apply to them. In the workshops I am currently leading, for example, I might spend the first part of the day going over the nuts and bolts of how to create a portfolio. Then I will give participants a few hours to actually create an entry, whether it is on their own, with a co-author, or with a group. Before we wrap up for the day, we will come back together to read one another's work, discuss what the learning process was like, and explore ways to implement it with students.

Many administrators are surprised that I give teachers a three-hour lunch, but the point, to me, isn't whether they are in the building; it is to have them come back with a finished product. Building accountability into the process (they have to share their work with the group) encourages them to use what they're learning. Most importantly, when teachers have time to explore and implement what they've learned, they also discover what works for them and how their students could benefit from the tool or process. The alternative is for teachers to sit and listen (or tune out) for a day-long professional seminar where no product was created and much of what is taught never gets put into action.

At the end of any professional learning day, I encourage participants to answer these two simple questions:

1. What did you learn today?
2. How will your students know what you have learned and benefit in their own development?

My goal is for every participant to be able to effectively answer these questions. No matter who is leading your professional learning days, I encourage you to use these questions to determine whether the time invested was well spent.

But maybe you are not an administrator and don't have the authority to reshape professional learning days in this way. First of all, if you see merit in what I am sharing, ask. I used to tell my staff, "I can't fix problems that I don't know exist." The worst that can happen is your principal or district leader could say no. The best thing that can happen is you have an impact on learning for your colleagues and yourself. We need to train ourselves to think: "What is the best thing that can happen?" You will start to see more possibilities than obstacles if you are willing to simply ask for what you want or need. So ask!

> **We need to train ourselves to think: "What is the best thing that can happen?"**

But they still might say no; now what? Using the digital portfolio example, consider how to learn with your students while they work on their process. Linda Yollis, an incredible educator from California, does "blog parties" where students all write together at the same time, in what I visualize as a Starbucks-type environment. Other educators I know do something similar, but they also write while their students are writing. What a great way to model your learning and grow yourself while you are with your students.

There are a ton of ways we can find our own spaces outside of school for growth in today's world. If you are a first-year teacher reading this book, you should be *soooo* much better as a teacher in your first year than I was (that is kind of a low bar, but still). You have access to so many more ideas directly related to what you do now than I ever did back then. For example, if you are a kindergarten teacher and are not following #Kinderchat on Twitter or Instagram, you are missing out on connecting with the wisdom of kindergarten teachers from schools all over the world. Here's a tip for finding resources to help you learn: Instead of asking, "Who should I follow?" on any social media, look for groups that teach your grade level or subject as a starting point. If you want to be part of a school that provides "world-class education," know that there is no better way to achieve your goal than to learn from people who do a similar job from around the world.

We have to make our own time for learning outside our professional learning days. Those days that are set apart for learning are important. But it is also a good practice to create space within the standard work day to dig into research, collaborate, share stories with colleagues about classroom and student success, and test ideas. In other words, we must be intentional about making time to learn.

Learning *with* Our Students

When I lead professional learning days, after I've shared some content and ideas, I like to ask for a couple volunteers to tell the group what their big takeaway was from the session. After they share with the group, they will share that same learning in a Twitter video that I tweet to the world. To be honest, the answers are often better in the video than they are to the group because the participants think more deeply about what they are sharing when they know strangers around the world might have the chance to see it. That is one benefit of this process but not the sole reason I am sharing it. After we create the video, I ask the group to share a video reflection of their own on Twitter, whether it is in a group, individually, or however they see fit. I ask them to share their reflection to their school hashtag and give them a thirty-minute "reflection break" so they have time to do the activity and connect with one another. Here is one key to the activity: I tell participants that if they have never created a video on Twitter, I won't help them. Then I share three words we do not say enough to our students: "Figure it out."

Those three words shock many teachers, but I use them as a reminder that I am not there to spoon-feed their learning. If they don't learn how to figure things out on their own, what will happen when I (the teacher) am not there? It is amazing to watch how different people in the group accept the challenge. Some immediately gravitate to their tech-savvy colleagues. Others go to a private space and start "pushing buttons" until they figure it out. Some put themselves in the video and some talk while "videoing" something else because they are not ready to put themselves out there. What is amazing is that after everyone makes their videos, we watch them and are invariably inspired by the ideas shared. And as the "teacher" of the group, I always learn something from a) how the participants learn and b) the ideas that are shared.

Even though I might be perceived as the "expert" by participants in the room, the purpose of these activities is to show that the experts are all around us. In our classroom, this means students can learn from the teacher, the teacher can learn from the students, and students can learn from one another. It is the embodiment of the Bill Nye quote, "Everyone you will ever meet will know something you don't."

In our classrooms, we have to be comfortable with the fact that we don't know everything. Admitting that reality and still being willing to learn, especially from your students, *doesn't mean you aren't an expert in your classroom*. It just acknowledges that our students bring gifts to the classroom. We can learn from them, a fact that, in and of itself, sometimes pushes our students to want to learn more. As someone who taught technology to all grade levels in my career, there is no way that I could know everything because technology changes so quickly. What you know about technology one day can change significantly with a simple "update." Because I *knew* it was impossible to know it all, sometimes I would ask my students, "Does anyone know how to _____?" Tapping into their knowledge was a way to save time *and* showcase their expertise. If a student knew a quick strategy that could save me time, why would I not learn from her? Sometimes students would know and help immediately, and sometimes students would see my question as a challenge to learn something quickly so they could show me how to do it. The intoxicating thrill of teaching the teacher empowers students and equips them with the ability to "figure it out" long after our time with them.

> ## The classroom as a whole is always way smarter than the teacher as an individual.

The classroom as a whole is always way smarter than the teacher as an individual. We need to be able to tap into the wisdom of our students to make us better now and to help them become better learners in the future. When we unleash the genius of the "whole" in our classrooms, there is no limit to what we can learn together.

Learning Is Not Just for Teachers and Students

I've intentionally used the language of learning *about* your students, *for* your students, and *with* your students as a means of connecting learning in these three areas for teachers. I generally use the term "learners" to refer to all of us, but in this case, I used "students" because, ultimately, that is who we serve. But the act of learning in schools must not be limited to teachers and students. School and district leadership must also embody this dedication to learning. In their article, "The Best Leaders Are Constant Learners," Kenneth Mikkelsen and Harold Jarche state the following:

> *Reinvention and relevance in the 21st century instead draw on our ability to adjust our way of thinking, learning, doing, and being. Leaders must get comfortable with living in a state of continually becoming, a perpetual beta mode. Leaders that stay on top of society's changes do so by being receptive and able to learn. In a time where the half-life of any skill is about five years, leaders bear a responsibility to renew their perspective in order to secure the relevance of their organizations.*[5]

Administrators can easily implement these ideas and swap the word "students" with "staff" or, even better and much more encompassing, with "community."

Administrators who learn *about* the community understand that every individual they serve is unique and brings different strengths and abilities to the table. Building relationships, tapping into these strengths, and unleashing the diverse talents of those we serve makes our community better as a whole. Just as is true in the classroom, our entire school community benefits when each person is empowered to share their unique abilities and talents with our community.

Administrators who learn *for* the community understand that personal growth benefits the growth of the community as a whole. Far too often, schools are held back by an administrator who knows too little, rather one who knows too much. This

> **Leaders must get comfortable with living in a state of continually becoming, a perpetual beta mode.**

doesn't mean administrators have to know everything (that is a dangerous narrative and unrealistic), but they do have to be willing to learn to serve their community and be vulnerable enough to admit when they don't know—but commit to learning to serve the greater good.

Administrators who learn *with* the community understand that they do not know everything, but their community as a whole might have—or be able to find or create—the solution. When administrators empower their colleagues to lead based on a variance of strengths, the entire community benefits. Great leaders know when to be great followers. Sometimes they need to lead from the front. Sometimes they need to guide from the side. Sometimes they need to learn from the back. And sometimes they need to get out of the way completely. If administrators can bring out the best in each learner in their community, they will help create a better community.

> ## Great leaders know when to be great followers.

"Learning" should not be reserved for teachers and students. It is the crux of what we do and should be embodied by all of the adults. If we are passionate about education, we will realize that learning has no endpoint; it is a continuous journey with many opportunities to explore.

Moving Forward

When I looked to hire teachers in my role as an administrator, a crucial characteristic I sought was something I called the "sponge factor." This trait was second only to a focus on relationships.

I am much more comfortable working with a teacher who is willing to learn and grow than one who thinks they have "mastered" teaching. Things will change in education and society, and someone who is not willing to evolve in their practice will eventually become irrelevant. In contrast, the person who is willing to continuously learn and evolve will always stay relevant.

Feedback is often the mechanism that helps us know when change is necessary. You know as well as I do, however, that there are people in every school who will happily listen to feedback, nod their heads in agreement, then go back to doing what they have always done. They may hear feedback, but they aren't open to it. They don't have the sponge factor. My question for you is this: Are you open to learning in a way that you would expect from your students? Are you open to feedback?

To determine whether a candidate I was interviewing had the sponge factor, I'd often say, "Tell me an area where you received feedback, and what you did to improve." This inquiry promoted a vulnerability that I believe is needed to be an educator. It also showed me whether the person was open to feedback and willing to do something because of the feedback received.

Learning is not a skill reserved for school; it is necessary throughout our lives. Some of the best-known entrepreneurs in the world, such as Oprah, Elon Musk, and Warren Buffet, ensure that they make time to learn and grow, as they know continued success in the future is dependent on what they are willing to learn today.[6] This skill is not only reserved for entrepreneurs, but also for any career and facet of life. As discussed in the beginning of

> **You can fight change, adapt to change, embrace change, create change, or lead change. No matter your choice, change is not going away.**

this chapter, my parents grew not only in the world of work, but as parents as well. I will tell you that I am a much better parent now than I was when my daughter was first born, and for the benefit of my kids, I will continue to grow as my parents did. We can always get better.

Here's the hard truth: You can fight change, adapt to change, embrace change, create change, or lead change. No matter your choice, change is not going away. Are you open to your own evolution as an individual and as a professional? I hope so. Keep learning!

Questions for Discussion

1. Growth is essential to our work as educators. What is something you used to do as an educator that you no longer do? Why did you stop doing it?

2. In what ways do you learn about your students and how does that shift your practice?

3. Share an area where you received feedback and used it to improve. What was beneficial about the feedback and how did it spark your growth?

Please share to #InnovateInsideTheBox

Part One
SUMMARY AND ACTIONABLE ITEMS

Each one of the previous chapters highlighted the elements that comprise the Core of Innovative Teaching and Learning. My hope is that the concepts and stories shared sparked ideas that will lead to action in your work with students as well as your work with colleagues.

Let these elements, beginning with relationships as the center of the core, serve as a compass as *you* create *your* pathway to innovative teaching and learning. But before we move into the next section where we'll focus on activities and implementation, take some time to evaluate where you are—both in your individual practice and as a school—and start a conversation about what you think might need to change to better meet the needs of learners and what is working well.

Although each element could be used for "teacher evaluation," it is meant to be less about that and more about conversations that lead to community actions impacting all learners. It is not realistic for any outsider, including myself, to determine what good teaching and learning should look like in your school or classroom. I don't know the specific needs of your community or the unique challenges of the individual learners in your classroom or school. But *you* do. Or at least you can when you use these core principles as your guide.

In your conversations with the people in your community, I encourage you to identify what's already working well and to define what improvements could be made. Use these templates to get the discussion started:

Conversations for the Community				
Core Principle	How do we define this for our school or organization?	What are some examples of what this looks like in our school or organization?	What are some examples of what this looks like in our classrooms?	How will we know this "Core" principle is having an impact on the learners we serve?
Relationships				
Learner-Driven, Evidence-Informed Practice				
Empowered Learning Experiences				
Master Learner, Master Educator				

If you are a teacher, you may not have formal authority to lead this conversation for the entirety of the school, but I hope you will use what you learn in this book to start a conversation with your administrators. I encourage you to look at each element we've discussed and reflect on how each connects to and guides your own work. Here is a sample template you could use to help you think about each "Core Principle" and what it looks like in your classroom:

Personal / Teacher Evaluation			
Core Principle	What does each core principle look like in my work and growth as a teacher?	What are some examples of what this looks like in classrooms?	How will I know this "Core" principle is having an impact on the learners I serve?
Relationships			
Learner-Driven, Evidence-Informed Practice			
Empowered Learning Experiences			
Master Learner, Master Educator			

And to the administrators reading this, if you want to embody and inspire innovative learning and teaching, I encourage you to take a few moments for personal evaluation. How do each of these core elements guide or show up in your work?

Personal / Administrator Reflection			
Core Principle	What does each core principle look like in my work and growth as an administrator?	What are some examples of what this looks like in my practice as an administrator?	How will I know this "Core" principle is having an impact on the learners I serve?
Relationships			
Learner-Driven, Evidence-Informed Practice			
Empowered Learning Experiences			
Master Learner, Master Educator			

All of these templates can be found at innovateinsidethebox.com.

If you are looking at having a conversation as a school or district on these concepts, you can use the above templates and have individuals fill them out for themselves before you discuss them as a group. This allows people to think about each area on their own to alleviate the pressure of coming up with ideas on the spot in a group.

The purpose of focusing on the Core of Innovative Teaching and Learning is to set the foundation to empower students in their learning. If we want to be effective in this process, we can't skip the learning to get to the teaching.

PART TWO

8 Characteristics
of the
Innovator's
Mindset

In Part One, we focused on the Core of Innovative Teaching and Learning as the foundation of your practice as an educator. Part Two, which focuses on the 8 Characteristics of the Innovator's Mindset, lays a similar foundation, but for our students. Here, Katie Novak will join the discussion as we examine each of these traits, discuss why they are important, and give examples of what this can look like in learning for our students today by implementing Universal Design for Learning (UDL). If Part One was setting the stage, Part Two is having students put on the production.

8 Characteristics of the Innovator's Mindset

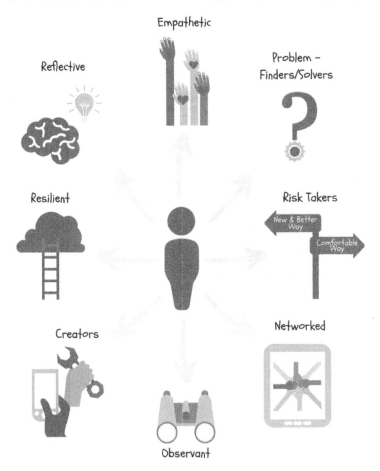

Empathetic

Reflective

Problem – Finders/Solvers

Resilient

Risk Takers

New & Better Way

Comfortable Way

Creators

Networked

Observant

I am really excited to have Katie co-writing each chapter in Part Two. I was lucky enough to hear her speak on UDL when we gave back-to-back keynotes at the annual symposium for the California Curriculum and Instructional Services Steering Committee (CISC) in 2017. Katie's philosophy and work within her own school district aligned perfectly with the "innovate inside the box" approach I've been advocating for the last several years: We can create empowering learning experiences for our students and have deep learning while doing well on traditional measures. Successful, innovative education does not have to be an either/or scenario. Katie's district embodies the idea that *how* you teach the curriculum is the innovation. Teachers are artists, and as John Steinbeck wrote, "Teaching might even be the greatest of the arts since the medium is the human mind and spirit."

I will open each chapter in Part Two with a focus on the *why* of each characteristic. Then Katie will share the *what* and the *how*. For the flow of the book and to keep writing true to our individual voices, you will see a simple "passing of the baton" symbol when we switch off. (Totally Katie's idea!) I feel blessed to write this book with her. I have learned so much about great teaching and learning from not only what she shares but also how accessible her ideas are.

And with that, I introduce Katie Novak, one of the most brilliant educators I have met and just an all-around amazing person.

Learners are not disabled. Curriculum is. Systems are. But kids are not.

This is the essence of Universal Design for Learning (UDL). Our task, as educators, is to design learning experiences where all students can be equally empowered, challenged, and supported. To do this, we have to be proactive about identifying and eliminating barriers that prevent inclusive learning and innovation.

George discussed a number of ideas around how we can navigate the barriers to learning in Part One: developing meaningful relationships, evidence-based practices, empowered opportunities to learn, and a learning community proactively working together to change our systems. Granted, relationships, strong pedagogical practices, and empowered learners alone won't be all that's required to create great systems, but we sure as heck can't change our systems without them. To give all students equal opportunities to learn, we have to be willing to examine our relationships, our own pedagogical practices, and the opportunities we create for students. Only then can we truly address some of the most significant barriers to high-quality education: inadequate resources, inequitable scheduling, curriculum bias, and state and federal policies, funding structures, and testing requirements that are not in the best interest of all students, especially those who are culturally and linguistically diverse.

We live in a world that embraces and encourages variability, the unique mix of strengths and weaknesses that make us who we are. We acknowledge this in restaurants where we enjoy diverse menus and clothing and shoe stores where we expect numerous styles and sizes. The school systems within which we operate, however, have not traditionally embraced variability. Many schools are still designed to provide a one-size-fits-all learning experience, which is neither accessible nor empowering for students or teachers.

As George noted in Chapter 3, "Nothing that has ever been deemed 'best practice,' however, works best for all students. Not. One. Thing." I'm going to turn that into a bumper sticker and slap it on the back of my Suburban.

"One-size-fits-all" learning disables some students. To make sure students have the opportunities they need to help them learn best, we use the three UDL principles to design experiences that provide options for students:

1. Provide multiple means of engagement.
2. Provide multiple means of representation.
3. Provide multiple means of action and expression.

The most basic example of the "one-size-fits-all" phenomenon, and how it can be transformed using the three principles of UDL, is a cookout. Imagine you're having a diverse group of twenty-five people over to your house for a cookout. Operation Perfect Cookout is a one-size-fits-all shabang that includes a free giveaway of matching red bikinis (a single means of engagement), cheeseburgers (a single means of food representation), and karaoke with a live Jon Bon Jovi cover band (a single way for guests to "take action" and express their love of summer). Party. Of. The. Summer.

Then, your guests show up.

Suddenly, you realize that your party plan missed the mark. You were so psyched to get everyone motivated to show off their summer abs in a one-size-fits-all bathing suit— and they have the audacity to complain!? *What do you mean that isn't your style? It looks fine!* Then your vegetarian, vegan, and lactose intolerant guests ask about food. Someone taps you on the shoulder, asking, "Do you have anything besides beef?" While you're trying to scrounge up some lettuce, you overhear another guest complain about being forced to sing along to "Living on a Prayer." (Who doesn't like "Living on a Prayer"?)

Here's the thing. In this scenario, you *know* that failure is predictable. Your party plans are riddled with barriers, and even a B-list party planner could tell you that. But, you argue, no one would *ever* throw a party with only one thing to eat or drink, or only one activity that everyone is forced to participate in. Instead, it would be planned with multiple options and pathways, just like we want our classrooms to be—hence the UDL principles.

UDL provides guidelines (specific strategies) regarding the types of options that students may need to learn. These guidelines also provide some party-planning support to help us proactively arrange for the perfect cookout. The UDL Guidelines are organized according to the three main principles of UDL that address engagement, representation, and action and expression. Think of these as the places where learners *may* face barriers to learning.

So if we use these guidelines when we plan our cookout, why don't we use them in so many classrooms and schools?

Often, it's because we believe or fear that we are required to take a one-way road to arrive at the formidable destination: "The Valley of Standardized Test" (cue the warnings from Chapter 2 on "Data-Based Decision Making"). This one-way path is paved with practice tests and other one-size-fits-all solutions for students who are anything but the same. Sounds kind of like the cookout from hell, doesn't it?

As Jon Mundorf, a tremendous middle school educator in Florida and one of the greatest UDL experts in the country, said, "I would rather teach in an *accessible* way for an *inaccessible* test than teach in an *inaccessible* way for an *inaccessible* test." We cannot test our way into increased test scores, and we sure as heck can't empower students or embrace our own creativity and art that way. Or as George likes to say, "You don't fatten a pig by constantly weighing it."

The Universal Design for Learning Guidelines

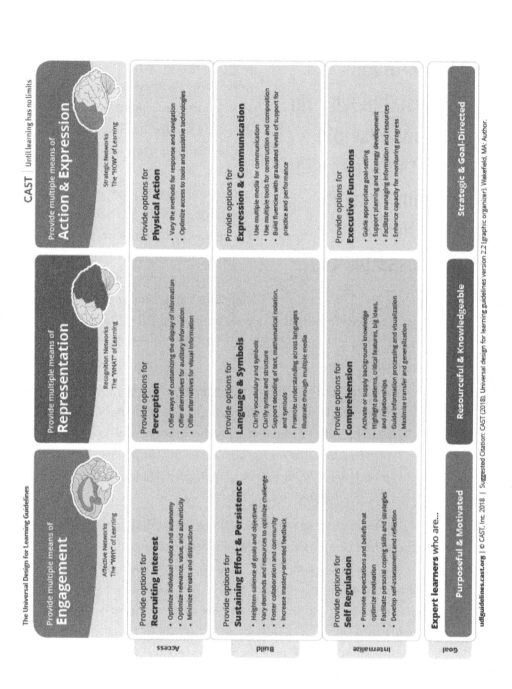

CAST | Until learning has no limits

Provide multiple means of Engagement

Affective Networks
The "WHY" of Learning

Provide options for **Recruiting Interest**
- Optimize individual choice and autonomy
- Optimize relevance, value, and authenticity
- Minimize threats and distractions

Provide options for **Sustaining Effort & Persistence**
- Heighten salience of goals and objectives
- Vary demands and resources to optimize challenge
- Foster collaboration and community
- Increase mastery-oriented feedback

Provide options for **Self Regulation**
- Promote expectations and beliefs that optimize motivation
- Facilitate personal coping skills and strategies
- Develop self-assessment and reflection

Provide multiple means of Representation

Recognition Networks
The "WHAT" of Learning

Provide options for **Perception**
- Offer ways of customizing the display of information
- Offer alternatives for auditory information
- Offer alternatives for visual information

Provide options for **Language & Symbols**
- Clarify vocabulary and symbols
- Clarify syntax and structure
- Support decoding of text, mathematical notation, and symbols
- Promote understanding across languages
- Illustrate through multiple media

Provide options for **Comprehension**
- Activate or supply background knowledge
- Highlight patterns, critical features, big ideas, and relationships
- Guide information processing and visualization
- Maximize transfer and generalization

Provide multiple means of Action & Expression

Strategic Networks
The "HOW" of Learning

Provide options for **Physical Action**
- Vary the methods for response and navigation
- Optimize access to tools and assistive technologies

Provide options for **Expression & Communication**
- Use multiple media for communication
- Use multiple tools for construction and composition
- Build fluencies with graduated levels of support for practice and performance

Provide options for **Executive Functions**
- Guide appropriate goal-setting
- Support planning and strategy development
- Facilitate managing information and resources
- Enhance capacity for monitoring progress

Access | Build | Internalize | Goal

Expert learners who are...

Purposeful & Motivated | Resourceful & Knowledgeable | Strategic & Goal-Directed

udlguidelines.cast.org | © CAST, Inc. 2018 | Suggested Citation: CAST (2018). Universal design for learning guidelines version 2.2 [graphic organizer]. Wakefield, MA: Author.

> ## "I would rather teach in an accessible way for an inaccessible test than teach in an inaccessible way for an inaccessible test."

Many students do not thrive in a one-size-fits-all system. The goal of school is not, and has never been, achieving high test scores and grade point averages. These are results that come when our students develop into expert learners. An expert learner is not a student who takes practice standardized tests ad nauseum, but one who becomes an expert at being an innovator by understanding the purpose of goals and standards and working toward those standards in ways that matter. In the book *UDL Theory and Practice*, written by the cofounders of UDL, expert learning is explained as follows:

> *Expertise is never static. Developing expertise in anything is always a process of continuous learning—practice, adjustment, and refinement. In the context of UDL, we focus on learning expertise: the lifelong process of becoming ever more motivated, knowledgeable, and skillful.*[1]

Expert learning requires students to have multiple pathways to meet their needs. The concept of expert learning encompasses all eight characteristics of an innovator's mindset, which we will highlight throughout Part Two of this book. If we want to improve teaching and learning, we have to create more equitable systems that empower educators and students to become problem solvers/finders, risk takers, creators, networked, empathetic, observant, resilient, and reflective. To accomplish this meaningful goal, educators need to design instruction using the three principles of UDL, so every student is empowered to know why learning is important, what it is they need to learn, and, most importantly, how to use the knowledge and skills to create something meaningful.

One of my greatest achievements as an administrator has been giving teachers the authority to create different pathways, using the principles of UDL to veer off the road that values sameness. It's not that we don't have to take standardized tests in my district. We do. But we don't map our journey on the backs of those tests. Instead, we embrace expert learning and the great adventures that come with it—think *Labyrinth* meets *Alice in Wonderland* meets *The Goonies* (All the best parts!). We are risk takers, we make mistakes, we practice resilience, learn from our failures, and, most importantly, we stick together and network with inspiring educators in our schools and around the world. And we expect the same from students. Through it all, we ensure that all learners, regardless of variability, have opportunities to work toward rigorous goals and standards in ways that are meaningful, relevant, and authentic. This is what it means to "innovate inside the box." The tests are a reality, but they don't have to dictate the pathways. It's the pedagogy that enables all students to develop new knowledge and skills they need to be successful.

Where do you start? Ditch the one-size-fits-all cookout. Then, turn the page.

Chapter 5
EMPATHETIC

*All it takes is one person to change
the world, and that person can be
you with a simple act of kindness.*

**–Natalie Hampton, student,
CEO of Sit With Us**

Empathy is defined as "the ability to understand and share the feelings of another."[1] Unfortunately, in some situations, this "ability" comes from wanting to ensure that others do not go through the same negative situation you may have experienced yourself.

Natalie Hampton developed the "Sit With Us" app in 2016, while still a student, after a terrible experience in her own school. She explains on the app's website:

Sit With Us was inspired by a miserable experience of being bullied in middle school. Apart from the verbal

*taunts and violence, one of the worst things was hav-
ing to eat lunch alone, and the embarrassment of having others see me eating lunch alone. After I changed
schools, whenever I saw someone eating lunch alone,
I would always invite the person to join the group.
Each time, the person's face would light up, and a look
of relief would wash over the person's face. Some of
those people have become some of my closest friends.*

*Sit With Us was born because I am committed to
making sure that other kids don't suffer as I did. I
believe that seemingly small, incremental changes in
the overall dynamic of a school community can bring
about change, so that everyone feels welcome and
included. I believe that every school has upstanders
like me, who are happy and willing to invite anyone
to join the lunch table. It is my hope, with people
pledging to be Ambassadors at their schools, that no
one will feel left out.*[2]

Because of Natalie's own experience, she created "Sit With
Us," which is a "free lunch planning app that promotes inclusion
in schools."[3] In her powerful TEDx Talk (bit.do/sitwithus), you
can feel her passion and empathetic nature. And you can hear
her commitment to creating spaces for other students to *not* go
through what she did. In Natalie's words, "Why did I get that second chance when so many other kids out there still suffer?" What
is truly powerful about what Natalie did is that she understood a
situation from experience. Instead of letting negativity and hurt
feelings hold her back, she used her experience as an opportunity
to help others in her community and around the world. She understood that making a positive difference in the life of one other person can change their outlook on life and make the world a better place.

Natalie embodies more than the characteristic of empathy. She exhibits other traits of the Innovator's Mindset: being observant, resilient, and creative. This is a reminder that these characteristics rarely work in isolation, but the focus on one can lead to a powerful combination of others. But there is a reason I am sharing "empathy" first. As Natalie reminds us over and over again, doing our best to understand the experiences and perspectives of others allows us to create better opportunities for *everyone*.

> # Doing our best to understand the experiences and perspectives of others allows us to create better opportunities for everyone.

The Difference between Empathy and Sympathy

Sympathy and empathy are not the same. In the article "Master This 1 Quality to Make Your Team Happier and More Productive," Jeff Miller shares this powerful story that distinguishes between the two words:

> *I'd taken a position at a school in Los Angeles. It was 1992. The school was just a few miles from the epicenter of the LA riots, which had taken place earlier the same year. The community was shattered. Many of my students lost their homes, and some lost family to gang violence related to the riots. I felt so sad for these kids, and tried to take it easy on them in the classroom.*

Until one day, when a fellow teacher pulled me aside and told me that my feeling sorry for these students wasn't doing them any good. And she was right. What they needed was not my sympathy, but my empathy. I needed to understand how they viewed school, how they viewed life and their future, and base my teaching on those understandings as best as I could though my life experience was very different.[4]

It is okay to feel sympathy for others, but when we do our best to understand the situation of others, it is more likely we are going to create opportunities to serve others. Empathy is what Natalie felt when she created Sit With Us. And it's a trait we must first embody before we can develop it in others.

Building Our Classroom Environments Together

In Chapter 1, I talked about the fact that designing your classroom with your students can be a way to build relationships with them. I can't tell you how many times I've made this suggestion to teachers and gotten responses along these lines: "Decorating the room is my thing. Don't take this away from me!" Even though they know it will save a tremendous amount of time, even though it could help the students take ownership of the classroom, some teachers still resist the idea of not decorating the room themselves *for* the students rather than *with* them. If that's you, maybe the following story will convince you to try this one simple strategy.

In my first year of teaching, the teacher across the hall put up an elaborate bulletin board with the name of every student entering her classroom on a penguin. She used penguins because she liked penguins. Feeling pressure to do the same thing, I created my own bulletin board and, because I loved basketball so much,

I put a picture of a basketball on the board with each student's name. My intention was to make the classroom a warm and welcoming place. Looking back, I can just imagine what the students who hated sports thought when they walked into my classroom: *I have a year with this guy?!* What if, instead, I had allowed my students to choose from a variety of things (sports balls, animals, flowers, balloons)? Or what if I had talked with them about the theme our room should take on and allowed them to share their interests before assuming they would be excited about basketball? My point is that when you look for opportunities to get to know your students and their interests and find a way to connect them to learning, you demonstrate empathy and create connections by caring about what they care about. Plus, it will save you a week of decorating. Better connections made in less time? Where do I sign up?

Empathy Is about Developing People, not Just Students

Developing empathy in ourselves and our students actually creates a better experience both in and out of school. According to Jordan Catapano in the article "Teaching Strategies: The Importance of Empathy," focusing on empathy helps us to develop the whole child:

> *The Yale Center for Emotional Intelligence likewise promotes its RULER program—a socio-emotional development curriculum for schools—to enhance the overall well-being of children. This promotes better individual and community health, leading to positive outcomes for academics and beyond. Socio-emotional development reduces a number of negative factors, such as hyperactivity, depression, anger, and aggression. In turn, this progress can improve*

children's attitudes toward school, improve rela-
tionships between students, allow for higher-order
instructional strategies, and create a more effective
academic experience.

Howard Gardner, who coined the Multiple Intelligence
Theory, also recognized the importance of interper-
sonal intelligence. It is what allows for our ability to
"understand the intentions, motivations, and desires
of other people." Empathy serves as a centerpiece for
socio-emotional development, as it focuses on stu-
dents understanding themselves and the perspectives
of any number of others.[5]

If we want students to do well in school and life, we must teach them and model empathy. Being empathetic helps us uncover and respond to needs, giving students insight into their purpose, which will not only lead to better academics but a better quality of life.

Proactively Eliminating Barriers

The East Bay Bike Path in Rhode Island travels 14.5 miles from India Point Park in Providence to Bristol. Each year, the frost heaves swell beneath the asphalt, which bulges the pavement in a pattern of speed bumps. In the spring, it's a disaster waiting to happen. These natural-made obstacles are dangerous, and almost invisible. To make for a smoother journey, empathetic Samaritans walk the path with cans of spray paint, identifying the barriers with large, fluorescent circles. When you can identify a barrier, you can avoid it.

Teaching and learning are a little like that. Universal Design for Learning (UDL) reminds educators to proactively design learning experiences by first identifying barriers so they don't derail the learning journey.

Cornelius Minor, lead staff developer at Teachers College and longtime educator in Brooklyn, famously said, "If reading is the inhale, writing is the exhale." If this is true, all of us would benefit from knowing what students have to "inhale" in order to "exhale" the "empathy advantage."

When teaching empathy, there are a number of barriers we need to be aware of so we can make them visible and easier to navigate for our students. The Making Caring Common Project,[6] developed by Harvard University, encourages educators to name the barriers to empathy before designing opportunities for students to build this important trait. They cite the most common barriers, including the fear of social consequences for helping an unpopular peer, stress, and stereotypes. Although we may not carry around cans of spray paint, when working with students to build empathy, it's important we highlight potential barriers and provide students with strategies to overcome them using the principles of UDL, so they can develop the mindset that will be critical for their long-term success.

Provide Multiple Means of Engagement

UDL reminds us to create a safe space for all learners. Individual variability is influenced by numerous factors, including lived experiences, culture, neurology, and background knowledge, to name a few. Being empathetic is critical to understanding different perspectives and embracing every learner. When we provide multiple means of engagement for learners, we can tap into their strengths, as well as help them see those of others. To do this, teachers need to reduce potential threats and distractions in the learning environment. One way to do this is to empower students to speak out.

- **Help Students Speak Out**. Oftentimes, students feel empathy but they don't take action. It is our responsibility to teach kids to speak out regardless of the fear of social consequences. Research suggests that when kids intervene in bullying situations, for example, more than half the time, bullying stops in ten seconds.[7] So why don't more kids speak out? It is possible they believe it wouldn't change anything, or they feel it would make things worse for them. Or they haven't learned how to speak out. Like Sit With Us creator Natalie Hampton, my second-grade daughter, Aylin, knows how to take action. When she was in first grade, a group of girls surrounded a boy with autism who was flapping his hands and mimicked him. She ran right over and announced, "Hey, ladies! If you want to mess with someone, you're gonna mess with me." A recess aide told me the story, and I wanted to buy her a pony. Not every student carries that same dose of diva, so we have to empower them with moral courage so when they feel empathy, they act on it. To instill or develop this empathy-courage muscle, we have to provide students with opportunities to stand up for or take action regarding something they believe in.

Strategies like class debates, presenting to younger students, speaking at school committee meetings and community events, and giving class presentations help students to practice speaking out. Teachers in my district often empower students to address injustices in public ways and encourage classmates to support them. Our recycling program at the high school is a result of a student creating a proposal and returning to the school committee meetings time and time again until it was approved. During the high school pep rally, the Best Buddies president got on the mic and talked about how some of his best friends and the greatest kids in the school had severe disabilities, and he wanted to recruit others to be a part of the club and join unified varsity sports teams. At our middle school, a small group of students started a diversity club. One (of many!) of their initiatives included designing and distributing posters and literature on the importance of embracing LGTBQ students. What opportunities do your students have to speak out in a public way against injustice?

Provide Multiple Means of Representation

Students need to understand what empathy is, and what it looks like, in order to understand the feelings of others. As educators, we need to use multiple means of representation to ensure all students can perceive and comprehend what empathy is, and what it looks like, in order to understand the feelings of others and to better understand their own feelings.

- **Teach (and use) emotional vocabulary**. UDL reminds us to clarify vocabulary and symbols, but our words have to incorporate more than academic vocabulary. To build empathy, students have to learn to read and identify emotions. First, however, they have to truly understand their own and others' emotions. Brené Brown, vulnerability and courage guru, created a list of core emotions.[8] (See the list that follows.) Provide opportunities to help students unpack these emotions; for example, have daily check-ins where they self-reflect and identify the emotions they are feeling, and allow them to have class meetings and small group discussions about how they feel.

Many elementary teachers hold a morning meeting that kicks off with a greeting and sharing. During sharing, kiddos share some news or information about themselves (could be highs or lows), and their partners respond with their thoughts and feelings. Imagine a kindergarten class where a little lovie shares that he lost his lacrosse stick, and his partner listens quietly and responds with, "Thanks for sharing. It sounds like you are *disappointed*. What are you going to do now?" Older students can share how they are feeling as they enter or exit the class. One of my high school history teachers, Tammie Reynolds, does emotional check-ins by assigning each student a magnet. As they walk into class, they grab their magnet. As they walk out of class, they place their magnet on a whiteboard under the correct emotion. She follows up with any student who needs support to model empathy.

Brené Brown's Core Emotions

- Anger
- Anxious
- Belonging
- Blame
- Curious

- Disappointed
- Disgust
- Embarrassment
- Empathy
- Excited

- Fear
- Scared
- Frustrated
- Gratitude
- Grief
- Guilt
- Happy
- Humiliation
- Hurt
- Jealous
- Joy
- Judgment
- Lonely
- Love
- Overwhelmed
- Regret
- Sad
- Shame
- Surprised
- Vulnerability
- Worried

- **Photo that represents**. As we unpack emotional vocabulary for students, it can be helpful to provide a visual as well as the definition—better yet, encourage students to find their own representations of what words like *empathy, anger, disappointment*, and *loneliness* truly mean. Ask students to bring a photo that represents the word under study. The beauty of marrying an exercise like this with the UDL framework is that we can build in all kinds of flexibility—think magazine cut-outs, drawings or paintings, or pics on their devices. When students are presented with multiple representations, they can begin to see that our experiences and world views are starkly different, and that is okay. Pair this activity with expectations for empathy by providing students with sentence starters like, "I'm *surprised* you brought in that picture as an example of loneliness because . . ."

Provide Multiple Means of Action and Expression

It isn't enough for students to understand what empathy is. They need authentic opportunities to practice being empathetic. UDL reminds us, as educators, to provide options for students to be strategic and express what they have learned. It is true with academic goals as well as with twenty-first-century skills. The following strategies provide support for learners to integrate empathy into meaningful coursework.

- **Practice perspective-taking.** To minimize the power of stereotypes, students need the chance to get to know and understand people who are wildly different from them. Teachers have numerous options for deconstructing stereotypes by providing students with multiple opportunities to work with diverse peers, both in and out of the classroom, and to "walk in someone else's shoes." In a seventh-grade ELA class, while reading an excerpt from *The Outsiders*, written from the point of view of the Greasers, students were given numerous options to create the same scene from the Socs' point of view. Although the Socs are rife with "rich kid" stereotypes, students had to look beyond those. How did the Socs feel when their best friend Bob was murdered? In a high school math class, students examine classmates' incorrect answers on assessments and answer the question, "Why did this person get this wrong?" They are challenged to examine the problem to determine why and where the student made an error. What did they believe to be true? It's a great activity to observe. Perspective-taking doesn't end with in-class studies of curriculum. How often do your students participate in service learning? Our high school English department, under the direction of the brilliant Kelly Cook, ditched traditional summer reading in favor of Summer Language Exploration.[9] Students have numerous options and choices to immerse themselves in language, but many of these assignments also build empathy. Not only are the students pumped to complete it, but parents, families, and the community participate as well. Check out a few of the options:

- Read to a blind person (through the Mass Association for the Blind and Visually Impaired), a child in a pediatric waiting room (through Reach out & Read), or someone else who would like to be read to on a regular basis. Keep a journal about your experience.

- Amass a bunch of old, random photographs from yard sales and flea markets. Use them to imagine a new story (Who are the people in the photos? What is the story behind each?), then organize them in some type of scrapbook/photo album format, complete with captions.

- Spend some time with your dog, cat, or any pet. If you don't have a pet, borrow one. Write a memoir from the animal's point of view. If you don't want to write a memoir, paint or draw the narrative, or write a song like Sting did in "Perfect Love . . . Gone Wrong."

- Humans of Groton (my town in Massachusetts!): Model your work after the Humans of New York. Find five people, take compelling portraits of them, and ask them to reveal something interesting regarding how they are feeling about their lives, which you will then turn into a caption. If it appeals to you, you can connect your subjects thematically or by location (workplace, travel destination, etc.).

Moving Forward

Empathy is a learned skill. If we want our students to practice empathy, we have to empower them to eliminate the barriers preventing the development of empathy so they can take action, clarify the language of emotional literacy, and minimize the threat of stereotypes by practicing perspective-taking.

Questions for Discussion

1. How can you increase moral courage by providing students with opportunities to speak out so they experience the importance of taking action when they feel empathy?

2. How can you use Brené Brown's list of core emotions to help create a foundation of emotional literacy and empathy in your students?

3. How can you design an assessment, like the Summer Language Exploration, where students work toward rigorous standards while also immersing in perspective-taking?

Please share to #InnovateInsideTheBox

Chapter 6
PROBLEM FINDERS-SOLVERS

We should strive not to have an answer for every question, but a question for every answer.

–Robin Pendoley

still consider our school's "Identity Day" one of the best days of my teaching career.

I've written about it in countless blog posts and in *The Innovator's Mindset,* and have spoken about it from the stage and with friends and colleagues. It was my favorite day as an educator and a principal for so many reasons—not the least of which is the story of a problem finder-solver I met that day.

On Identity Day, each learner in our school set up a space, like a science fair table, to share one thing about which they were passionate. My assistant principal at the time, Cheryl Johnson, organized the day and made sure it wasn't limited to students; staff also participated. The connections made on that day, and in the days following, contributed to us growing together as a learning community. I know that, for myself, learning about the passions of each person I served helped create connections beyond just that of "school."

Although I love all of the stories I could share from that day, one about a fifth-grade student named Marley is particularly relevant for this chapter. Marley had Tourette Syndrome and, although she wasn't teased by anyone at school for her tics, she felt that people were uncomfortable with them. She decided that on Identity Day, she wanted to give her classmates and other students in the school an opportunity to learn directly from her about something that she had a deep understanding of from her experiences with the condition. Marley knew the issue was that people didn't really understand Tourette Syndrome. She believed if she gave them the opportunity to learn directly from a person they knew who had Tourette Syndrome, not only would they become more understanding but they would embrace her for her differences and feel more comfortable being around her. I had no clue that Marley had chosen this, and when I walked into the classroom and saw the attention and interest she garnered in her project, tears welled in my eyes. It was a powerful moment. When I later asked if it was okay to share her story on my blog, Marley was excited for me to share it. Educators from all over the world commented on the blog because they were moved by her story. Then Marley herself commented:

> "Thank you sooo much for all the support and, yes, I am proud of who I am! And I'm not afraid to show the world. I'm looking forward to sharing all my knowledge with the world when I am older! Again, thank you soo soo much and I hope you have learned

that you shouldn't hide who you are and you should be proud of who you are."

Marley identified a problem and leveraged it to create a better experience for not only herself in our school but for everyone with whom she interacted. Even though this happened years ago, I still feel a sense of pride for this young lady who made an impact on people both in and out of our school community. I believe that a leader is someone who has the ability to move people forward in a positive direction. Marley, thanks to Cheryl Johnson and her teachers, was able to show her ability to move people forward on this simple, powerful day.

I truly believe that *the best way to develop the leaders of "tomorrow" is to give our students opportunities to lead today.*

> # The best way to develop the leaders of "tomorrow" is to give our students opportunities to lead today.

Ensuring Students Find Problems That Are Meaningful to Them

Focusing on developing our students as leaders is something I have believed in since I became an educator, but I struggled to find specific, effective strategies for doing so. It's easy enough to say we want our students to "change the world," but I wanted to find ways to go beyond talk and tangibly shift the focus in education—to help students become leaders because of school rather than in spite of it.

I then read about an idea from Ewan McIntosh, the founder and CEO of design consulting firm NoTosh, regarding "problem-finders." Although the concept had been floating around for a while, Ewan brought it home for me with this simple quote:

> *Currently, the world's educational systems are crazy about problem-based learning, but they're obsessed with the wrong bit of it. While everyone looks at how we could help young people become better problem-solvers, we're not thinking how we could create a generation of problem-finders.*[1]

The goal is not to develop our students as people who provide solutions to well-known problems. There is probably way too much of that in the world as it is. This is about helping students seek out problems that are meaningful to them and then finding ways to solve or respond to those issues. If you care deeply about the problem, you are more likely to find a meaningful solution while also enjoying the process.

A *Business Insider* article titled "The 10 Most Inspiring Inventors under 18"[2] highlights powerful examples of young people who created solutions to issues that mattered to them—solutions that are helping to make the world a better place. Although I would love to share all of the stories, two really stuck out to me.

Kylie Simonds, at age eight, had a sore throat. Upon visiting a doctor, she was diagnosed with cancer. Not wanting to be seen with "clunky, ugly IV poles," she invented backpacks for kids that carried all of the necessities for her medical needs while still being stylish and something a young person would want to carry around.

Kenneth Shinozuka, at seventeen years old, invented SafeWander, "a wearable wireless sensor that sends an instant alert on your phone when the wearer starts to get up from the bed or chair, even if you are far away."[3] This was built in response to worry that his "grandfather's nighttime wandering could lead to a dangerous fall or injury."[4] It didn't just make the person wearing it safer, but based on some of the reviews, it actually made the caregiver's life better as well:

> *SafeWander is an absolute MUST if you, as a caregiver, want to maximize your patient's safety while getting a good night's sleep! Before SafeWander, I would always sleep with one eye open just in case my mother got up and started wandering around the house in the middle of the night—a dangerous scenario for a myriad of reasons. But now that I can attach SafeWander to her pajamas, I can go to sleep knowing that I will be awakened at the first lifting of her body from her mattress! I can literally be in her bedroom before her feet hit the floor.*
>
> *Thank you, SafeWander! As far as I'm concerned, your invention should be the Invention of the Year!"*

> —Colin Swift

Both of these young people experienced a problem in their own lives and created a solution that not only helped them but also made an impact on others around the world. They came up with answers that, honestly, I would not have thought of in a million years. This serves as a reminder that age is not a barrier in making the world a better place.

Age is not a barrier in making the world a better place.

What Moves You to Action?

Angela Maiers, a former teacher and founder of "Choose2Matter," makes a subtle but important distinction on how we can actually become problem-finders by not following our "heart" but following our "heartbreak." In Angela's words:

> *Finding your passion, surrendering to your **heartbreak**, is really about finding what really moves you. Discovering what ticks you off and breaks your heart may be the first step in that direction.*

> *Here's why:*

> - *It identifies what you find interesting. When something truly breaks your heart, there is no doubt that you find it compelling enough to hold on to.*

> - *It uncovers a cause you long to be called for, what some call your "life's purpose."*

> - *It unveils a process that you can and will want to use to learn the skills you need to succeed and brings you closer to getting there.*

> - *It brings congruency, bringing what's inside you in closer alignment with what's outside you. When you believe that world out there needs what you've got, it becomes the exact motivation you need to propel forward and make change happen.*

> *And in my experience, following a heartbreak, whether it is your own or the world's, is the single most effective way to help individuals, organizations, and the world discover what they were meant and called to do.*[5]

When I first read about following your heartbreak as a way to lead students, my middle school and high school years flashed in front of my eyes, and I thought, *Why would we ever want to put anyone through that?!* But Angela shares this idea in a way that actually helps us to focus less on ourselves and more on finding solutions, big or small, that can make a difference in our world today. With the narrative that is being projected on young people in so many ways that they are the most "narcissistic" generation ever (which has probably been said about every generation of young people by the generation directly preceding it), encouraging problem-finding is a powerful way to help guide our students to see themselves involved in initiatives that are bigger than themselves. To get started, go back to the idea we discussed in Chapter 3 when we talked about creating empowered learning experiences; start by having students ask questions. Lots of them.

The Magic of Feedback

As George shared above, "If you care deeply about the problem, you are more likely to find a meaningful solution." This is truly the essence of UDL. All kids can, deserve to, and will learn at high levels if we are willing to recognize and eliminate the barriers and problems that prevent learning. And goodness knows, we, as educators, have been trying. But barriers still exist. Luckily, we have hundreds of little warriors and future problem-finders who are on our side and can help us identify and eliminate those barriers.

Students spend an incredible amount of time at school, and for many of them, this time, as Angela Maiers stated, is heartbreaking despite our best efforts. I still remember teaching what I thought was a fabulous lesson on poetry and noticing that one of my students was creating intricate paper cranes out of sticky notes. I squatted down and asked him why he wasn't following along. He looked at me deadpan and replied, "I'm sorry. I have to make these cranes because what you're doing is painfully boring. No offense."

Touché.

What could I do? I asked the class to tell me the truth, and I promised I wouldn't be upset. "How many of you think this is painfully boring?" Every hand shot up. We laughed together, and I dramatically threw my papers in the air. "Okay, let's start over," I said. I was a good sport about it, but the fact that my students thought the lesson was "painfully boring" was heartbreaking—for them *and* for me. And I needed to fix it. Here's the thing: I'm not alone.

According to research, 66 percent of surveyed students reported being bored in every class or at least every day in school. Of these students, 98 percent claimed that the material being taught was the main reason for their boredom, 81 percent thought their subject material was uninteresting, and two out of three students found that the material lacked relevance.[6] This is the mother of all problems, and UDL provides us with guidelines to solve this.

One way to foster authentic, meaningful communication in students, while also helping to hone their problem-solving abilities, is to ask them to give feedback about the problems they face during the school day. Sometimes, the problems that students face will be personal, like how Marley didn't feel like her classmates were comfortable with Tourette Syndrome. Other times, they can affect the whole class, the school, or the district. Right now, a number of high school students in my district have created a proposal to change the start time of the high school. Representatives come to school committee meetings to report research on the benefits and speak to administrators to determine flaws in their proposals, and then they collaborate and return. They found a problem, and they are fighting for a solution.

But why can't we embed some of this problem-finding into our curriculum? We can! Here's how to start:

Multiple Means of Engagement

When designing learning experiences, UDL principles can help us to make learning relevant, authentic, and meaningful to students. In order to recruit student interest, we have to provide them with learning experiences that ignite and foster effort and persistence. When we provide opportunities for students to identify barriers and problems that matter, and empower them to address those barriers with support from our system, we are a step closer to building purpose and motivation that they will carry with them long after graduation.

- **Ask**. Ask students to solve the problems that prevent them from being successful in school. Every day is an opportunity to ask students to find and solve problems. Ask students to tell you what is wrong with the schedule and collaborate in groups to propose a new one for administration. Ask elementary students why bullying occurs and how to prevent it. Ask them why they are so bored in school and how to fix it. Ask them what they are passionate about and what problems they want to solve. And once they have identified problems, use curriculum and instruction to help solve them. Empower them to explore research, create proposals, design and deliver presentations, create prototypes for inventions, run pilots and trials, and monitor their progress along the way.
- **Have Faith**. When I learned about UDL, I resisted. For a fleeting moment, I saw myself being replaced. What would the classroom be if I wasn't the star, standing proudly like

an Oscar recipient as my students watched in awe? The answer? The classroom would be empowered. Students would be collaborating to analyze Shakespeare by Skyping with students around the world, arguing about the use of rhetoric in political campaigns, and taking their learning into the community to create anti-smoking campaigns, to begin academic competition teams, and fight to find their way in the world. They gave me feedback and challenged me to prove myself against Siri, to admit my mistakes and learn from them, and to help them carve a path to a place that didn't exist. I couldn't do this alone, nor could they do it without me. My role as an educator became even more important when I stepped out of the spotlight because it required me to craft and personalize my message to all students instead of throwing it out in a "one-size-fits-all" ball and hoping they all caught it. So have faith that encouraging students to find and solve their own problems will, in turn, solve many of yours.

> So have faith that encouraging students to find and solve their own problems will, in turn, solve many of yours.

Multiple Means of Representation

Providing students with exemplars is an effective way to build student comprehension. Multiple exemplars and representations help students to build background knowledge, build understanding, and, most importantly, begin to see what is possible.

- **Share.** Students need to see examples of other kids their age solving problems. Elementary students may think they don't have the ability to make large-scale change.

Middle and high school students may think the world isn't listening to them. It's simply not true. One great example of the power of student voices is the Groton-Dunstable Peace Club. The club was founded by my late colleague, Betsy Sawyer, and is credited as making the *Big Book of Peace*. Here's how they explain the project:

> *Pages for Peace is the project of a group of public school students devoted to the idea that kids CAN make a difference in helping to create a more peaceful world. To prove our point, our after-school writers' club at Groton/ Dunstable Middle School in Groton, Massachusetts worked for twelve years to build the biggest book in the world about peace. We began by writing letters, asking people worldwide to send us their messages of peace. Over time we received thousands of letters, poems, and pieces of artwork from all around the world, and we began work to compile them all into the Big Book. That is when we knew that this project had the potential to spread an inspirational message, and the world's largest book about peace was born. The book includes over 1000 pages of content, with each page measuring an incredible 12 feet tall and 10 feet wide.[7]*

Hello, *Guinness Book of World Records!* These kids have solved a problem—granted, it took twelve years, but that is the awesome sauce of growth mindset.

Multiple Means of Action and Expression

The goal of UDL is to empower students to become purposeful, motivated, resourceful, strategic learners. When we can provide students with multiple pathways, time, and support to find and solve problems, they can begin to internalize what it means to be a problem-finder, then set out to solve problems on their own.

- **The UDL Progression Rubric.**[8] The Progression Rubric, designed with my colleague Dr. Kristan Rodriguez, is a self-assessment tool that encouraged educators to reflect on their UDL practice. The rubric helps to identify what UDL looks like when implementation is emerging, proficient, and progressing toward expert practice. When progressing toward expert practice, each guideline notes that students are empowered. Specifically, educators are called to "empower students to self-reflect, self-assess, and create personalized action plans to achieve their identified goals. For example, encourage students to reflect on how much time and what kinds of resources they need to perform selected tasks and then encourage them to make personal due dates and task lists to reach their goals."
- **What I Need.** If you find that your schedule is a problem, and it doesn't allow for personalized time, fight for a schedule that allows students to get the time they need to work toward their goals. Many school districts I work with, including mine, schedule a WIN ("What I Need") block to allow students to schedule intervention, enrichment, or advisory and club activities. Having enrichment time where teams of students can work to solve their passion problems, "genius-hour" style, helps students to personalize their learning journey.

Moving Forward

If we want to make the world a better place, we have to empower students to find problems that matter to them. We must also equip them with the skills and time to solve them. Although there are numerous problems to find outside of school, UDL is all about identifying and eliminating the issues that impede teaching and learning. Collaborate with your students to identify and eliminate school- and system-wide barriers that prevent inclusive education so all students can find passion, purpose, and success during the school day.

Questions for Discussion

1. Think of one problem that is meaningful to you as an educator. How can you model the practice of problem-finding to your students while solving something that is significant to your own world?

2. If you asked your students to identify the most heartbreaking aspects of school, what do you think they would say?

3. How could you design learning experiences that would help students to solve the problems that prevent them from being successful in school?

Please share to #InnovateInsideTheBox

Chapter 7
RISK-TAKERS

Life is too short to be scared and not take risks. I'd rather be the person that's like, "I messed up," than, "I wish I did that."

—Justine Skye

I first started teaching in 1999, and because I had a little bit of experience with technology in university, my first full-year position included a designation of teaching "computers" to all students in our K–7 school. A little experience with technology at that point seemingly was a lot more than what was normal.

Instead of just focusing on technology, I wanted to meaningfully integrate technology into different subject areas. At the seventh-grade level, one unit was dedicated to poetry. Being the "cool" teacher I was, I thought, *Kids don't want to learn poetry! Why not teach song lyrics? That is awesome.*

In the beginning, my students loved the unit and the opportunity to find songs that they were interested in. Breaking down the lyrics in search of hidden meanings proved to be a powerful exercise that felt meaningful to the students. (One major problem with my approach to this unit was it didn't consider that maybe at least some kids *did* want to learn poetry. I tailored the learning experience to what I thought was interesting rather than asking what mattered to the students. Obviously, my thinking has evolved since that first year, but that is not the point of the story.)

One day, in our computer lab, I wanted to give the students the opportunity to dig deeper into one of my favorite Canadian bands. The school had the slowest dial-up internet you could imagine (Remember twenty minutes to download one song on Napster? That slow.) Yahoo! was the browser of choice at the time, and I encouraged my students to search for the Canadian band, "The Barenaked Ladies." As I watched my students slowly hunt and peck their way around the keyboard, a terrifying thought crossed my mind: *Wait a minute . . . they might not find the band!* Luckily, a main power switch provided power to every computer in the lab. I immediately shut down every computer and acted like I had no idea what had happened to the power. (Who could have imagined that slow internet would have been such a lifesaver?!) Still playing dumb, I told my students that something must be wrong with the computers. We went back to our classroom and studied poetry.

That experience of trying to do something different, and having it go horribly wrong, froze me for a *long* time in my career. I am ashamed to admit that, for far too long, I stuck with lessons that were easy for me rather than trying to get better for my students. I eventually got over my fear and moved on. Looking back on that experience, though, helps me understand why so many people in education focus on what could go wrong. The problem when that is our focus, however, is we lose sight of what we could do right.

Risk-taking does not fit in with the concept of perfection, but in the pursuit of making sure everything is just right, we give up so much learning and growth.

How Do You Look at Risk?

Risk shouldn't be a scary thing. When I use the term *risk-taking*, I am not sharing it in a way that is focused on doing things that would harm our learners. I define *risk* as moving from a comfortable average in pursuit of an unknown better. When you read it like that, it is not as daunting.

Risk can come not only in what we do but also, sometimes, in the things we don't do; for example, I have put a big focus on my physical health over the last two years. Every morning, instead of looking at my phone and getting sucked into the rabbit hole of social media and email (which I used to do), I have decided that I need to exercise and run before I do anything else. I have noticed that taking care of my physical health has made a tremendous impact on my mental health as well. But understand this: Every morning that I get on that treadmill, there is a risk that I might fall off and sustain some type of injury. Knowing that running carries an innate risk, I could choose to use that time in the morning to stay in my warm and comfortable bed and get an extra sixty to ninety minutes of sleep or get a jumpstart on my email for the day. But there is a risk with that cozy and comfortable choice as well. It is just not as evident at the moment. Forgoing exercise in the morning over time will definitely lead to increased health risks as I get older. Knowing that what I put off today could harm me significantly in

> **I define risk as moving from a comfortable average in pursuit of an unknown better.**

the future, I choose instead to take the risk of doing something now to get better for the future.

> Knowing that what I put off today could harm me significantly in the future, I choose instead to take the risk of doing something now to get better for the future.

A desire for comfort can also hold us back in the classroom as we rely on our past lessons or on traditional practices. Please understand that I do not equate "traditional practice" with "bad practice," and I have no issue with traditional methods of teaching—*when they work for students.* As I said earlier, whatever individual learners need to succeed is where we begin. Innovative teaching and learning is about creating opportunities that empower all learners to thrive, which usually means we have to vary our approach since our students are varied in their interests and goals.

I do, however, have an issue with "bad" or ineffective practice, which includes doing things we know don't work for our learners. This isn't done out of malice but because we, as educators, are comfortable with the process; we have a plan and the materials, and we know what to expect—even if it isn't much.

Not moving away from those ineffective practices, whether in the classroom or at the school or district level, is a major risk we take with our students each day. We risk students being disengaged and not seeing the value of their education, and when that happens, we miss out on their contributions and the genius they keep hidden and don't have a chance to develop. We can't just do things because we have done them before. Think of things like homework or award ceremonies. I am not saying either is bad, nor am I saying they are good. That is for you and your team to decide. What I am saying is that a lot of these things are still done in our schools not because they are necessarily effective in serving our students, but because we have always done them. I think it is always good to revisit "traditional practices" and ask, "Does this work for our students today?"

What Happens When We Stick with the Default?

Do you use Internet Explorer? For years, it was *the* browser that school IT departments installed on every computer. From a very early point in my career, I did everything I could to get around our default system. I put either Firefox or Google (and later Google Chrome) on all of our computers because they were faster and had so many more options than Internet Explorer.

In his book, *Originals: How Non-Conformists Move the World*, Adam Grant notes that this search for something "better" for our students and their web searches is actually less about being "tech savvy" and more about not accepting the "default" in our lives. As Grant explains, to put Firefox or Chrome on your computer, you had to show some resourcefulness and initiative. Those qualities are what meaningful risk-taking is about. In contrast, a lack of willingness to seek out better options (simply submitting to using an Internet Explorer, for example) could be a microcosm of how we are willing to "accept the defaults in our own lives," Grant explains.[1] If we are willing to be comfortable with "that's just how it is" in our own work, why would we expect our kids to make the world better? Without risks, we stick with the default, whether it is good for us or not.

You Need to Jump in First

My brother, Alec Couros, PhD, a huge influence in my educational career, shared a powerful video with me of a child talking to herself before taking a ski jump off a large ramp. The video is shot with a GoPro camera, which allows you to feel the anxiety the child feels as she takes this leap for the first time. It is nerve-wracking just to watch! As someone who has only skied a few times in life, I feel nervous every time I watch the video. The child, who is skiing with an adult and a friend, is working up the courage and then finally takes the jump. What a rush! The first-person angle of the camera has you flying through the air and soaring with adrenaline until the child gets to the bottom of the hill and exclaims, "Just the suspense at the top for the first time freaks me out. That's the only thing; it's so fun! Sixty [meters] seems like nothing now! *WHOOO!*"

What I love about the video is it serves as a reminder that we were once terrified to do so many of the things we don't think twice about doing today. That could range from driving a car to posting a tweet. It is always good to remind ourselves that we were once at the top of that hill, terrified to jump.

Besides the rush of emotion, there are a couple moments in the video I especially love. The adult who is there eases the child's anxiety by talking through the jump, giving insight into what to expect. To me, it exemplifies that we are far too often pushing our kids down the hill with no experience ourselves, and just hoping for the best. This is not a good strategy. Wisdom from our own experience is beneficial to guide our kids, even in things we did not necessarily "grow up" with. It is okay to allow our children to try different things for the first time on their own, but this is happening too much in our world today—especially as they explore social media and technology on their own—and a lack of familiarity in these learning experiences may be more of a hindrance than a help.

Another moment I love in the video is when the young friend with the child says something amazingly profound: "The longer you wait, you'll be more scared." Isn't this so true of things that we put off in our lives—personally or professionally? The more we hold ourselves back from jumping in, the more we make excuses why we shouldn't even try in the first place.

As discussed earlier in Chapter 4, we need to understand the opportunities that exist in learning for our students today. When caregivers ask us to explore a new type of learning for their children, we have to be able to speak to the children's needs and the new methods from the viewpoint of both a teacher and learner. Being a master learner mitigates unnecessary risk for our students and brings us comfort as we try to explore new things. The risk should always start with us; to be the best example for our learners, we have to jump first. It is from that learning we are then able to successfully guide our students and communities through troubled areas.

Students Grading Teachers: The Ultimate Risk

When I taught seventh-grade English, I took a big risk. I decided I would ask my students to grade me as their final project. I shared all the standards I was expected to teach throughout the year, and I laid out the challenge: "If you don't know what these mean, and if you don't remember the learning experiences that taught you why these things are important, I haven't done my job. Grade me accordingly." Note: This exercise is not for the faint of heart.

We devoted two class periods to the project, during which they worked collaboratively in groups to reflect on the year and my strengths and weaknesses as a teacher. They reviewed their portfolios, had conversations with me and one another, and asked clarifying questions. Once they reviewed everything, they had to assign me one final grade, which they could present to me in an artistic representation, written rationale, or multimedia presentation. I'm proud to say I only failed a single standard overall. "Explain the function of phrases and clauses in general and their function in specific sentences." I still remember the presentation when Lally stood up on behalf of his group and solemnly told me, "We all agree that you may not actually know what this standard means." I burst out laughing. I assured them that I did, in fact, understand exactly what it meant, but I clearly didn't teach it very well. Lally looked me straight in the eye and said, *"But do you?"* Gosh, I love kids. The next year, I promise I upped my grammar game.

Here's the thing: By not asking students for their assessment of my teaching, I would have still been taking a risk. Yes, it would have been more comfortable to assign a final project and convince myself I had nothing to improve. But because I believe educators should take the road of empowering student voices (we work for them, after all), we need to give them opportunities to speak their minds and provide feedback about the impact of our lessons.

An expert learner, by definition, is a risk-taker. Failing and mistakes are part of the learning process. When we embrace that fact, we are more willing to dive in the deep end of improvement. The book *UDL Theory and Practice* notes that "expert learners know how to solve problems flexibly, to adapt or change course when they make mistakes, and to fine-tune their own strategies for even better performance."[2] For me, asking students for their feedback was a way to fine-tune my teaching. As a teacher, I can't think of too many strategies that will empower your students as much as opportunities to be authentically heard and to be a part of the improvement of their learning environment.

Provide Multiple Means of Engagement

If we want students to take risks, we have to model risk-taking. We also have to create an environment that minimizes the threat of taking risks. The problem is, we likely think we have created an environment of risk-taking, but our perception isn't enough. We have to ask our students. This is the epitome of risk-taking—taking the risk of asking your students if you really encourage risk-taking.

- **Give feedback surveys.** We have to be vulnerable enough to ask students questions about our teaching and the environment we create for them to learn. The following prompts are from the Massachusetts Department of Elementary and Secondary Education (MA DESE) Model Feedback Surveys.[3] Teachers can provide these prompts to students and ask them to rate their level of agreement, selecting from: strongly agree, agree, disagree, and strongly disagree. DESE posts surveys that are developmentally appropriate for K–12 students, as well as surveys that administrators can give to teachers. Imagine providing students with prompts quarterly about the teaching and learning environment. The results of this practice will help you to answer the question: *Have I created an environment where risks are not only encouraged but expected?*

Example Prompts

- My teacher demonstrates that mistakes are a part of learning.

- My teacher encourages students to challenge one another's thinking in this class.
- Students push each other to do better work in this class.
- The level of my work in this class goes beyond what I thought I was able to do.
- When I am stuck, my teacher wants me to try again before she or he helps me.

Provide Multiple Means of Representation

The UDL guidelines remind us to activate background knowledge and to pre-teach prerequisite concepts through demonstration or models. Whenever you can model the importance of the innovator's mindset, or provide opportunities for students to model for each other, you are closer to building true understanding.

- **Share your reflection**. Taking the risk to collect student feedback is one thing. Sharing the results with them is another. The first time, you will feel a little like the child cliff-jumper with the GoPro! But soon, it won't be as scary. Will you share the feedback results and your goals with your students as a model of the importance of taking risks? Parents of students? Close colleagues? The department? Your evaluator? Remember when sharing the feedback that multiple means of representation is key. Don't just verbally share the results—show them charts, share your goals for improvement, and allow time for questions and answers. I observe classes all the time when teachers address a class saying things along these lines, "Thanks so much for the feedback last week. Up on the projector are the results from the Google Form. As you can see, when responding to the statement, 'When something is hard for me, my teacher offers many ways to help me learn,' 30 percent of you disagreed. So this is something I really want to work on. I'll be checking in every day to see how I'm doing." Your students, their parents, and colleagues can be amazing accountability partners.

- **Empower Students to Seek Feedback.** Once you model the importance of feedback, it's critical to empower students to ask for feedback about their work and share the results. This can be done through peer feedback and assessment, critique protocols, the setting of Big Hairy Audacious Goals (BHAGs), or sharing their failures, and what they learned from them, on failure walls.

Provide Multiple Means of Action and Expression

When we design learning experiences using the principles of UDL, we empower students to create and act on plans to make the most out of their learning. To make this journey worth it, we have to eliminate the barriers that prevent students from taking risks. Try the following strategies to help them embrace the magic of risk-taking and the inevitable failure that often comes with it.

- **Risk pass.** Take action and ask students what they would love to accomplish in school if failure wasn't possible. Would they write and perform a song? Start a diversity club? Design and teach an entire lesson? Produce a video? Run for student council? Ask the principal if recess could be longer? If they need inspiration, make a list and ask them to check off all the things they would love to accomplish but are too nervous or scared to try. Then, write them a pass to try it. And embrace their effort when they do. I gave my seventh graders risk passes, which guaranteed them full credit if they gave full effort, regardless of the quality of the project.
- **Failure Portfolio.** A *New York Times* article, "Do You Keep a Failure Résumé? Here's Why You Should Start,"[4]

highlighted the importance of keeping track of failures and lessons learned. The article notes, "Whereas your normal résumé organizes your successes, accomplishments, and your overall progress, your failure résumé tracks the times you didn't quite hit the mark, along with what lessons you learned." Consider collaborating with students to create failure portfolios where they can set BHAGs (big, hairy, audacious goals), monitor their progress, and share their outcomes, successes, and, most importantly, their failures and what they learned from them. Understand the importance of this process is not highlighting the "failure" as much as it is the journey and growth through the process (more on this in Chapter 11). Students can share their risk-taking process with classmates through peer review or share the link with authentic audiences in the community to help build a culture of risk-taking, reflection, and the ultimate reward of success.

Moving Forward

To be a master learner with an Innovator's Mindset requires risk-taking. To create an environment where all students can take risks, teachers have to be willing to "jump off a cliff" and partner with students to determine how their teaching either encourages or hinders taking risks and making mistakes. Only then can teachers remove the barriers that prevent students from launching from the comfortable into the unknown.

Questions for Discussion

1. If you knew you could not fail, what risks would you take to improve teaching and learning for all students?

2. What will you give yourself a "risk-pass" to do in order to improve teaching and learning for all students?

3. How will you "jump off the cliff" to ask for student feedback about your teaching and learning environment?

Please share to #InnovateInsideTheBox

Chapter 8
NETWORKED

*Social media is like water. You can either
let us drown or teach us to swim.*

–High School Student

The above quote came from a student during a professional learning day that included approximately 50 percent educators and 50 percent students. It was in response to an educator in the room who had argued all day that students didn't need to use social media because "I didn't have it when I grew up, and I turned out fine" (an argument I hear often). Our students have the opportunity to connect in ways that many of us didn't have as kids, ways that we must help them navigate and leverage. Logically, we all know this, but it took a student's voice (and the courage to share it) to change this teacher's perspective. (Kudos to the teacher for listening to this student's perspective and changing his practice as a result!)

Sometimes the voices that most resonate with educators are those of students. This is one reason the concept of "networked" is crucial both to innovative teaching and learning as well as to helping students develop an Innovator's Mindset. Sharing, hearing, and acting upon the voices of others is essential to progress. I intentionally chose the term "networked" for this characteristic, as it alludes to the value of connecting and collaborating with others face-to-face, as well as online and in real-time or "different-time" situations. Being networked isn't about just face-to-face or just social media or just online communities. It's about connecting.

A perfect example of what it means to be *networked* is Mari Copeny. You might know her as @LittleMissFlint on Instagram or Twitter. Or you might not know her at all, but you should because she plans to run for the United States presidency in 2044.[1] I first became aware of Mari Copeny when she was eight years old. She was living in Flint, Michigan, during the water crisis and became one of the biggest advocates in the community. She has shared her voice on social media and leveraged her connections in the "real world" as well on that community's behalf. In 2018, she connected with the non-profit Pack Your Back to donate 10,000 backpacks filled with supplies for students in the 2018–2019 school year[2] and, in the same year, collaborated with Pack Your Back again to provide 135,000 bottles of water to residents of the community of Flint.[3] In Copeny's words: "You're never too young or too small to change the world."[4]

The Importance of Digital Leadership

Because of the stories of young people like Mari Copeny, I started focusing on the term "digital leadership" and informally defined it in 2013 as "using the vast reach of technology (especially the use of social media) to improve the lives, well-being, and the circumstances of others."[5] What I have found in many schools, especially when talking about social media, is that the practice is often to talk more about "don'ts" than "do's," such as, "Don't bully people online." The problem with this focus, as my friend Michelle Baldwin explained to me, is that the brain doesn't process the word *don't*. Think of it this way: If I say "don't walk," what do you visualize? My guess is you didn't visualize sitting, but walking.

My focus has always been on sharing with students what they *can* do, rather than what they can't. I have never focused on anti-bullying as an educator, not because I don't think bullying is wrong but because we set the bar for leadership by raising our expectations for students. If you focus only on "don't be a bully," the best result of your actions is "don't be a horrible person." I choose to aim much higher.

I wish I would have realized the negative impact of the word "don't" years ago, before addressing 2,000 high school students in an Indiana high school gymnasium. Focusing on "digital leadership," I started the day by encouraging the students to get on their phones and share their thoughts with me on Twitter. I reminded them that their teachers were there, "so don't post anything inappropriate." As you can guess, the first three tweets, sent from three anonymous accounts in the room, were directed not only to me but also to the hashtag for all the other students to see, and were absolutely horrendous. As an advocate for students connecting and learning from one another and the world, my gut reaction was still, "*Shut this down!*" Then I caught myself: *Should I really shut it down because of three kids out of 2,000?* Which, by the way, schools do often. A kid breaks their arm on a playground? Shut down playgrounds. A teacher does something wrong? Create procedures that will punish all teachers in the future. We often punish the majority for the actions of the few. I do not want to be that person.

So I tried to redirect the group and altered my talk on the fly. I said, "When I was a teacher, you as a student could have had a tremendous impact on me. Do you know how I measured that? If I saw you outside of school, would I cross the street to talk to you? If I did that, I knew you had an impact on me, and I hope I would be that for you. Hopefully, we can be that for each other."

In about a minute, a student named Dida tweeted about the effectiveness of my presentation. I called him out and thanked him for his impact on me in that moment. Understand, I was terrified. I knew zero people in this room and had anonymous accounts attacking me. Dida used his platform—exemplifying digital leadership—to redirect his peers. Within minutes, positive comments flooded the hashtag. They ranged from how effective my presentation was to "I like your sweater." Dida and these students taught me something that day: We need to make the positives so loud that the negatives are almost impossible to hear. They also reminded me that by focusing on what *to* do, rather than on what not to do, we raise the bar for students and increase the likelihood that they will meet and exceed our expectations.

> **We need to make the positives so loud that the negatives are almost impossible to hear.**

This does not mean we don't listen to challenges and criticism; those things are crucial for the growth and development of individuals and organizations. Dida reminded me, and modeled himself, that being solution-focused is often the best way to move forward.

What Do You Bring to the Group?

The concepts of *networked*, and even digital leadership, have so much to do with connection and collaboration. But, as always, there is more to the story. In the examples that I've shared of Mari and Dida, we can see that they used their digital platforms in a way that demonstrated positive leadership. But how did they get to the point that they had enough influence to bring focus to an important issue or change the direction of a conversation? What was the process that led to them knowing their message, their voice, and being brave enough to share? My guess is that someone encouraged them to develop their voice and equipped them to share it.

Collaboration is about tapping into and bringing out the strengths and differences of the individuals in pursuit of a common goal. As we discuss the importance of collaboration in our work, it's necessary to remember that the work of collaboration itself begins before we ever say a word or share a tweet. Many people, myself included, need to do some processing in isolation before bringing ideas to the table. That's why, in the summary of Part One, I suggested giving people time and space to develop their own thoughts about the core elements of innovative teaching and learning before coming together to discuss them as community. This is based on the idea of *brainwriting* not *brainstorming*. Brainstorming is the practice I most often see put into practice when groups collaborate. The trouble is that, in these sessions, not everyone will or even has the opportunity to share their contributions. In the article "Brainstorming Doesn't Work; Try This Instead,"[6] the author Rebecca Greenfield notes that "in most meetings with traditional brainstorming, a few people do 60 to 75 percent of the talking." She suggests having participants write about their ideas, questions, and solutions before coming together with the group. That's brainwriting, and it helps ensure that people have the opportunity to process their ideas and develop their thoughts.

The end result is that what gets shared in a group setting is more meaningful than if people are just spouting off random ideas—or not sharing any because 1) they aren't sure what they think, or 2) they can't get a word in edgewise because the conversation is dominated by people who like to talk (regardless of the amount of thought behind their words).

Everyone's voice matters and is valuable to the process and outcome of what you are trying to achieve—as a class, a school, or a community. As Susan Cain says in her book *Quiet*, "There's zero correlation between being the best talker and having the best ideas,"[7] so it is imperative we find a way to help bring out the voice in others in ways that are beneficial to them and the group. Brainwriting is one strategy that helps to ensure that every voice is empowered and heard. You never know where the best idea will come from, but by networking with a diverse range of people and sharing well-thought-out views, we can collaborate more effectively and find the very best ideas to move our classrooms, schools, and communities forward.

I want to share one more thought about collaboration before passing the baton to Katie. As a principal, my first hire was for an assistant principal. To this day, I would say it was the best hire I made in my career. Cheryl Johnson, who recently retired, is an incredible thinker, teacher, and doer, and is a passionate advocate for students. I had the same passion for students, but I will tell you that Cheryl and I didn't always agree. We had different viewpoints and experiences, and I knew this before I hired her because we had worked together in a previous school. We shared the same vision, but our different approaches and insights were exactly the reason I hired her. I didn't need someone to think like me; I already did that. I wanted someone who thought differently and would connect with people who may not have felt as comfortable connecting with me. I needed her voice and perspective so that I could learn and we could grow as a community. The power of learning from those we disagree with is we can often find some of the best answers to move forward as a community (both in school and in life) where we are willing to understand that some of the best answers are in the middle. By finding ways to promote, hear, and act upon voices different from our own, we tend to grow not only as a group, but as individuals.

Fostering Collaboration and Community in UDL

Early in my career, I had the opportunity to be a part of a project called Elevating and Celebrating Effective Teachers and Teaching (ECET2).[8] Funded by the Gates Foundation, the purpose of the project was to bring together innovative educators from across the country to share best practices in teacher-led professional development and networking. Attendees included state teachers of the year, as well as a diverse group of teachers who were committed to deconstructing practices and systems that created unequal outcomes for students: think sipping coffee while pondering a problem of practice with teacher, writer, and spoken word poet Clint Smith (@ClintSmithIII) and Boston middle school teacher/teacher-travel guru Lillie Marshall (@WorldLillie) at the same time. Mind blown.

Providing time for collaboration and learning is one of the key ingredients that makes an ECET2 event successful. Teachers spend their days helping students learn. ECET2 offers teachers the time and space to grow as they learn from inspiring speakers and from one another. Furthermore, ECET2 provides a platform that enables this collaboration to continue long after the convening.

I attended ECET2 conventions in cozy lodges in Snowbird, Utah, and beachfront hotels in La Jolla, California, but two days in edu-paradise would never have been enough to support my professional growth. The face-to-face time was critical to begin the work, but we needed to continue to network together after the convening. Given that we were spread across the country, we needed digital platforms to do it. The same is true for our students.

In my district, the AP Spanish teacher and world language coordinator, Jacquie Liebold, wanted students to create their own project-based final exam. She empowered them to use their fluency in Spanish to do something meaningful in our community. They had the autonomy to make connections, create an authentic project, and determine how it would be graded. Within a couple of days, I had high school students emailing me, asking for permission to drive to an urban district a half hour away to teach Spanish to second graders three days a week. When we provide students with authentic opportunities to network and drive their own learning, it's a hell of a ride. (As an aside, 88.2 percent of these students scored a 3 or better on the Spanish AP exam.)

Networking isn't a "one-and-done," and it shouldn't be put aside to focus on standardized testing. It needs to be woven within the fabric of teaching and learning. UDL reminds educators to foster collaboration and community to build purpose and motivation. That collaboration and community, however, isn't limited to between classroom walls, as my own high school students showed me. To make a difference, they needed to get out of the classroom. As George said in the *Innovator's Mindset,* "Our world today is participatory; sharing should not be the exception in education but the rule." This needs to be true both inside and outside the classroom walls.

Provide Multiple Means of Engagement

UDL reminds us to provide numerous options for students to be networked. When we foster collaboration and build communities that can give and receive mastery-oriented feedback, we create the conditions to drive toward success. The following strategies provide multiple opportunities for students to build both attention and commitment in the learning environment.

- **Foster cogen dialogues**. One research-based strategy that fosters collaboration between students and teachers is co-generative dialogues—or cogens—advisory groups of four to five students who are empowered to "speak their minds, identify specific examples to illustrate where improvements can be made, and identify examples of exemplary practices or counter-examples of those that exemplify a need to change."[9] Cogen dialogues, coined by Christopher Emdin, a professor at Columbia University, empower educators to create co-constructed classroom communities. Imagine creating groups of diverse students with the power to improve education in the school. You can provide students with sentence stems to offer feedback like, "It would be cool if . . ." or empower them to respond to prompts like, "I always feel safe in this school," with reasons why or why not, so you can begin to address barriers to their learning. What an amazing way to give student council or an advisory period a twenty-first-century makeover!

Implementing cogen dialogues allows students to make an incredible impact on your practice. You can do this with a single group of students or create multiple groups within your classroom. Peter Anderson, a middle school English teacher in Virginia, started his cogen groups the old-fashioned way: bribery. He writes in his blog, "Ever since September, I've been meeting with a select group of students to receive feedback on my classroom instruction. Wooed by free 7-11 donuts, five students spend every Monday's lunch period sitting in a circle and telling me what's working and what could use some improvement. The students take the time seriously and view our weekly meetings as important."[10]

- **Family Hook-Ups.** We all know the importance of collaborating with families, but many schools don't go beyond back-to-school nights and mystery readers. *Every* student caretaker has something to offer. Find out what it is. When parents and caretakers are completing back-to-school paperwork, give them homework. Ask them, "What is one thing you are really good at and you could teach me?" If they don't return it, call them. Assure them it could be anything—cooking empanadas, deep sea fishing, kickboxing. Then, throughout the year, make it a practice to network with them and get them in the classroom, in person or virtually. When I taught seventh grade, one of our units included an excerpt from *The Old Man and the Sea*. I know next to nothing about fishing, but Tim's dad did. He came in with his fishing equipment and photos and videos of his best catches, and sparked interest and answered questions about deep sea fishing.

Invite the community in and allow families to inspire, teach, and learn with their students. It doesn't matter if they are four years old or twenty, your students need to know their families can be a part of meaningful teaching and learning. You can even extend this beyond student families. Contact elected officials, local business owners, and former students!

Provide Multiple Means of Representation

Here are some ideas that will help to build an environment where students can use available resources and connections. Knowing how to find and tap into connections will empower them to build their knowledge and use resourcefulness, both of which will optimize their contributions when they have opportunities to collaborate and network.

- **Doodle or Google**. The concept of "brainwriting" to activate prior knowledge is critically important to ensure equity in participation. A barrier to "brainwriting," however, can be that students don't have adequate background from which to draw. When teaching, set a timer for three minutes and encourage students to "Doodle or Google." Essentially, this allows them time to brainwrite, write questions, look up information if they need background knowledge, or take visual notes. If students have phones or devices, it's an easy opportunity for them to build basic background and get inspiration for the collaboration that follows. This will prevent the possibility of "I didn't have anything to brainwrite."

Provide Multiple Means of Action and Expression

Let's take the ideas of "Doodle or Google," cogen dialogues, and family hook-ups and bring them all together to discuss the power of providing students with the opportunity to take action and create their own networks with each other, the teacher, and with learners around the world.

- **Network Hook-Ups**. Allow learners to "Doodle or Google" to make sure they have the background information they need to collaborate in a meaningful way. If you want them to take action and create their own networks, you have to think about collaboration on a bigger scale. Want to empower students to create meaningful dialogue about prison reform, for example? Empower students to "Doodle and Google" as you design your lesson. Their task? Find people who could contribute to the class's understanding of the real-world issue. These could be professors, bloggers, community members, or other students. The purpose of the brainwrite is to network and plan a unit. It's like the cogen dialogue meets the internet. The 2014 National Teacher of the Year, Sean McComb, does just that in his Teaching Channel video, "Making Learning Personalized and Customized."[11]

He asks students to create a list of topics they care about, then students find someone online who's working on the topic they've chosen. The video highlights a group of students interviewing an expert in prison reform. One student on the video clearly understood the purpose: "[We] try to get a view of someone who actually experienced it, not just trust what the internet says."

- **Find a Sister Classroom:** Consider hooking up with classrooms working on similar activities (through Skype, for example) or find "sister classrooms" to comment on student blogs or portfolios. It's like giving pen pals a twenty-first century makeover! And these "classrooms" don't have to be cohorts of students. Link up with retirement communities, Council on Aging groups, and local non-profits to network, ask questions, and share student work.

Never underestimate the power of planning units with students. We can't talk about collaboration without highlighting the need for the partnership between students and teachers. When we can foster a shared commitment to planning learning experiences with the power of technology, we can give every student the power to plan, collaborate, and, most importantly, work together with people who would otherwise be out of reach.

Moving Forward

Although it's important to foster collaboration in the classroom, it's vital that students can learn from diverse partners remotely to ensure ongoing collaboration with learners who have different perspectives and so much to offer. The world is too vast to limit collaboration to within our classroom or school walls.

Questions for Discussion

1. How can you use cogen dialogues to collaborate with students about how to create more opportunities for them to work collectively and network in meaningful ways?

2. Families provide an amazing resource to foster collaboration and networking. What strategies can you implement to network with families and provide opportunities for students to learn and share the best of the people who are closest to them?

3. How can you design learning experiences that empower students to take action to create their own networks?

Please share to #InnovateInsideTheBox

Chapter 9
OBSERVANT

What you focus on expands, and when you focus on the goodness in your life, you create more of it.

–Oprah Winfrey

When our daughter was born, we wanted to give her a unique name. Growing up as a "George" in a Greek community, where it seemed everyone was named George, I never knew when someone was talking to me or the kid beside me. More than a few times, I have had people say when they meet me that their grandpa was named George or their dead cat. Maybe the cat was named after grandpa. Who knows?

My wife and I wanted to spare our little girl that confusion. We also thought that, in a world where everyone we teach will be *Googled* at some point, an uncommon name would be of benefit to our daughter because it would make her easier to find. We settled on the Greek name "Kallea" (meaning beauty and goodness). We loved the sound and the rarity. We still love the sound, but since our daughter's birth, I have met an endless number of "Kalleas" (some with different spellings, but all essentially the same name). On our first family trip, we stayed in a house on a street named "Kalia" in Hawaii. The name "Kallea," which we had never heard before our daughter's birth, is *everywhere*.

You've probably experienced this phenomenon yourself, and you know it doesn't just happen with names. You buy a new car and love it, then realize you see that same make and model *everywhere* you go. No, this isn't a "Truman Show" stunt being played on you. The reality is that those cars (and kids named Kallea) were there all along. You are simply more aware of them now because they matter to you. What you focus on tends to find you.

> ## What you focus on tends to find you.

Becoming Observant in a World Full of Noise Is More Valuable than Ever

As more and more information is thrown our way and the "noise" becomes louder, the ability to slow down, listen, find great information, and make deep connections is becoming much more essential; for example, if you are new to a social media platform, finding relevant and meaningful information feels a lot like trying to find a needle in a haystack. It seems impossible and overwhelming. The skill of finding nuggets of wisdom and powerful links to information is one that you develop over time. And it's a skill that directly relates to two of the "21st Century Literacies" as presented by the National Council of Teachers of English (NCTE):[1]

- Manage, analyze, and synthesize multiple streams of simultaneous information
- Create, critique, analyze, and evaluate multimedia texts

In short, these literacies rely on our (and our students') ability to be observant of the *right* information—not *all* the information. Being observant requires critical thinking as we decide and decipher what to listen to. It also relies on the skill of making and acting upon connections. Ideas like "Genius Hour" in education were derived from ideas in the business world, such as Google's "20% time." But it took someone who was observant of the business world, and who could make the connection between what worked there and what could work in schools, to iterate the practice in a way that was meaningful to classrooms. As a side note, we often talk about what education learns from the business world, but every educator reading this knows that the business world could learn a ton from education—not only in ways of learning, but in how schools have always been able to figure out how to do so much for the people they serve with so few resources. It is impossible to throw endless amounts of money at a problem in education, and businesses could learn a ton from the resourcefulness of teachers.

How Do We Become More Observant in Our Passions?

When I started to focus more on the idea of "innovation in education," I began to see it everywhere. Whether it was seeing how someone ran a business, or while watching a YouTube video, or even listening to music, ideas on "innovation" started popping up everywhere. I noticed them because I was looking for them and because I wanted to make the connections between innovation elsewhere and innovation in schools. Here are a few things that helped me see and connect more:

1. **Listening more.** I can't remember who condescendingly made this point to me when I was younger, but it sure did stick. "You have two ears and one mouth, so you should listen twice as much as you talk." Sometimes the loudest noise we hear is our own voice. The ability to listen and take in information is crucial to our own growth. We can't make connections unless we hear the idea in the first place.

2. **Slowing down.** We are so quick to speak and share ideas, when, sometimes, we should simply be processing. Ever wonder why some of the best ideas come to mind when you're in the shower? There's actually science that backs it up. According to Harvard researcher Shelley Carson, the dopamine release not only helps creative ideas come to your mind, but the "distraction may provide the break you need to disengage from a fixation on the ineffective solution."[2] Stepping away from a problem helps to make the ideas more clear.

3. **Cutting out as much unnecessary negativity in my life as possible.** Constant interaction with negative people is bad for your health and intelligence. According to the article "Why Negative People Are Literally Killing You (and How to Protect Your Positivity)" by Elle Kaplan, research has proven that "even a small amount of negative brain activity can lead to a weakened immune system."[3] And according to Dr. Travis Bradberry, "negativity compromises the effectiveness of the neurons in the hippocampus." One of the best pieces of anonymous advice I have heard when dealing with negativity is this: "Don't take criticism from someone you wouldn't take advice from." Often, the negative people around you will stop talking if you refuse to get sucked into their spiral.

What does the last point on being surrounded by negativity have to do with becoming more observant? I noticed that when negative thoughts (and sometimes people) crept into my mind, I would lose focus on what was important. For example, when I go out for a run, the longer I run and the more tired I get physically, the more negative self-talk creeps into my head and can sabotage my goals for the day, week, year, even life. A trick that I was taught by a student-teacher was to say the word PACE ("Positive Attitude Changes Everything") in my head over and over again until I regained my focus. It seemed cheesy at first, but then I started using it, and it has helped tremendously in keeping me focused on what is important. A cluttered mind cannot think clearly.

> **A cluttered mind cannot think clearly.**

Finding Meaningful Connections in Unique Areas

Mikaila Ulmer, who is a "social entrepreneur, bee ambassador, educator, and student," has a unique story of how she created a great opportunity from two totally separate events. Mikaila is the young founder of "Me and the Bees Lemonade," a company that is "selling 360,000 bottles of her lemonade a year, with stockists including upmarket supermarket chain Whole Foods Market." As of writing this, Mikaila is fourteen years old, but she started her company at a much younger age with the encouragement and support of her family. Here's how Mikaila tells her story:

> *When I was just four, my family encouraged me to make a product for a children's business competition (the Acton Children's Business Fair) and Austin Lemonade Day. So I put on my thinking cap. I*

thought about some ideas. While I was thinking, two big events happened.

- *I got stung by a bee. Twice.*

- *Then my Great Granny Helen, who lives in Cameron, South Carolina, sent my family a 1940s cookbook, which included her special recipe for Flaxseed Lemonade.*

I didn't enjoy the bee stings at all. They scared me. But then something strange happened. I became fascinated with bees. I learned all about what they do for me and our ecosystem. So then I thought, "What if I make something that helps honeybees and uses my Great Granny Helen's recipe?"

That's how Me & the Bees Lemonade was born. It comes from my Great Granny Helen's flaxseed recipe and my new love for bees. So that's why we sweeten it with local honey. And today my little idea continues to grow.[4]

Mikaila's story exemplifies the characteristic of being observant. The experience of being stung by a bee and connecting that (somehow) to her Grandma's lemonade and creating a business—one that is not only successful monetarily but also environmentally aware—is a powerful example of how, if we are open and searching for them, ideas can grow into something bigger than we could ever imagine. One of my favorite parts of this story is that, although the idea came from Mikaila, her parents have had a major impact on her and given her the support she needs to be successful in the venture. "We're considered co-CEOs because I make decisions that my parents wouldn't make, and my parents make decisions that I wouldn't make," Mikaila says. "Also, I am young . . . I know I don't know everything, and so I am definitely going to take their advice and opinions into consideration."[5]

This is a reminder that, although our students are brilliant, adults guiding them in a positive manner can lead to greater results.

UDL and Expert Learning

Being observant is the core of the scientific process. Research defines *observation* as "the interactions between the sense organs and the attributes of objects that bring us data from the external world that are processed under the control of our mental activities and placed in our consciousness."[6] My translation: Learning, innovation, and success require observation.

UDL requires all students to become expert learners, learners who are motivated, purposeful, knowledgeable, resourceful, strategic, and goal-directed. When thinking about the skill of being observant, there is a strong link to the importance of being resourceful. Too often, we design our classrooms so students become knowledgeable, but how often do we ask them to be resourceful? As an example, when working with teachers, many note that time is a barrier to designing UDL lessons. This is because traditionally, teachers feel like it's their job to bring all the resources together in order for students to learn.

> **Although our students are brilliant, adults guiding them in a positive manner can lead to greater results.**

Consider this scenario: You want your students to understand the causes of World War I, and you want to provide multiple options for them to build that knowledge. You probably feel like you have to be the one poring over primary source resources, watching endless YouTube clips, and finding reputable internet sites so you can provide them with a menu of reliable, valuable sources. If you did that every day, you'd sure as heck be out of time. But even though that lesson may, in fact, result in students who are uber-knowledgeable about World War I, they never had the chance to be resourceful or observant. So how can you give your lesson design process a UDL makeover? Put those students to work!

Multiple Means of Engagement

Before I learned about UDL, I was always busting my tail to create engaging lessons. I was working way harder than the cherubs who sat in front of me. Then, UDL rocked my world and those two words, "choice and voice," became a part of everything I did. Not only did I ask students how they wanted to learn, but I empowered them to help me to design lessons that eliminated barriers for them and their classmates. To do this, I asked them to be observant.

- **Co-create lessons.** Before diving into a unit on *The Old Man and the Sea*, I asked students to go online to find projects, activities, and lessons that aligned to the work we were doing. They were encouraged to network with friends, ask their parents for advice, and examine standards. *Together*, we built lessons that aligned to standards and empowered them. Mikaila Ulmer observed problems and used resources to address them, but she did that alongside her parents. The same process can be done with lesson planning, and, I promise you, you'll never have more buy-in, empowerment, or achievement than when the power of observation is shared with all your students.

- **Help them slow down.** With so much to cover and so little time, it may feel like a bit of a rat race to design and deliver lessons. The reality, however, is that we have to schedule downtime for our students. The Pomodoro Technique reminds us that for every twenty-five minutes of active learning, students should be given time to reflect, think, take a break, stretch, or breathe. Another idea is to become a master at meditation. One of my high school colleagues facilitates a short meditation before she gives exams. When she asked for feedback about the practice, every student appreciated the time and believed it helped them slow down before the test. Providing students with time to quietly brainstorm, observe, and be mindful is critical to promote self-regulation and coping.

Multiple Means of Representation

UDL reminds us of the importance of learner variability. When we embrace variability and inclusion, we recognize that there is not one means of representation that will be optimal for all learners; providing options for representation is essential. This often includes scaffolding skills and providing students with opportunities to build a vocabulary that is meaningful to them. Being observant will certainly help students with both of these tasks.

- **Scaffold listening skills.** Students need to know the difference between the various types of listening in order to use them effectively and observe the world around them. Teach them the difference between active listening and cognitive listening and provide them with numerous options to practice both.[7] *Active listening* requires listeners to physically display emotion (That's why empathy is so critical!), ask questions about what is being said for clarification, and contribute appropriate explanations and comments. Students should practice active listening when working in groups, sitting at lunch, and having class discussions.

Cognitive listening is a little more intense. When cognitively listening, students make inferences and generalizations, take notes, and formalize what they learned to make learning more permanent (read: they are observant and question *everything*). When I am networking with colleagues, I actively listen. When I attend lectures, I cognitively listen. I know the difference—and that's critical to the way I am able to observe and process information, as well as to my ability to make connections and take action. Help students to learn the differences and then use the skills to their advantage—because both types of listening are great for being observant, when you use them well! Create a class bulletin board with visuals and examples of when to use each type of listening because, let's face it, if you pull out a spiral bound notebook when hanging with friends and push back on everything, you may be waiting a while for a prom date.

- **Make your own vocabulary lists**. Knowledge is all around us. Consider asking students to pay attention to it. Instead of coming up with a one-size-fits-all vocabulary list, ask students to spend a day and truly observe the world around them with an ear toward vocabulary. They can eavesdrop on conversations, read the newspaper, listen to the radio, focus on signs and song lyrics, and use closed captions on their favorite streaming shows. Empower every student to bring in a list of five words that they heard, or read, and didn't quite know the meaning.

Not only does this provide them with personalized vocabulary lists but, because they gleaned them from the world around them, the words are culturally responsive and linguistically appropriate. I imagine Mikaila Ulmer (Me and the Bees Lemonade) would glean words like *alarm pheromone, candy plug, intermediaries, acquisition,* and *merger.* And I'm willing to bet her classmates' words are going to be quite different! Empower them to own the words and then, for the rest of the week, ask them to listen for them because they are everywhere.

Multiple Means of Action and Expression

As educators, it's tempting to think we have to design all the lessons to teach students how to be expert learners. But the magic of expert learning in UDL is that students can be a part of the design and delivery of learning experiences. Put those babies to work!

- **BYOR (Bring Your Own Resources).** Empower students to seek answers to essential questions by bringing their own resources. For example, students may choose to read culturally sustaining literature that speaks to them while studying geography regions (E-books and audiobooks count as reading!). In math, they may choose to view educator lectures from around the globe or watch Khan Academy to prepare for a lesson. Encourage students to use virtual reality and augmented reality to observe people and natural habitats and phenomena. Using Google Cardboard, some middle school students in my district toured the tundra biome from the back of a snowmobile while others laid on their bellies and pored over library books. The power of this activity is that students bring in the resources that help them to build understanding and answer questions. And there are numerous places where students can access resources even if they don't bring them from home. Provide students with time to explore your school library, share/swap resources with one another, or use school devices to access resources online. As an educator, you don't have to be the one to create a menu of options to explore. Empower students to observe and use all the resources available at their fingertips. It helps them to create strategies, then notice and observe the resources that are most appropriate for them.

- **Assign observations**. When I taught seventh grade, we read an article about littering and pollution. One student noted how gross it was to see cigarette butts on the school grounds. "There aren't any cigarette butts around here," we argued. But an impromptu walk and the power of observation showed us there were thousands. The students were incredibly fired up, which led to letter writing campaigns, news coverage, and some sparkling-new trash bins around campus with signage to remind everyone not to smoke. When my twins were in kindergarten, they learned that the drip-like mud castles in the grass were in fact piles of earthworm poop (seriously, Google it). After learning about the phenomenon, the students were given time to walk around outside, silently, to admire the worm poop. They came home from school elated and, to this day, I can't walk in the grass without looking for it. When you ask students to observe, you make the invisible, visible.

> **When you ask students to observe, you make the invisible, visible.**

174

Moving Forward

To become expert learners, students have to become more observant of and interact with the world around them. Countless resources and strategies are available *everywhere* to help them build inspiration and enhance motivation and reach their goals. We have to design learning opportunities that leave room for students to observe the world around them, find their passions, and ask their own questions so their learning experiences aren't cluttered with "one-size-fits-all" resources that pave a path for them.

Questions for Discussion

1. How will you allow students to co-design a lesson with you using their powers of observation?

2. Try the vocabulary activity yourself! Observe the world around you today and identify five words that you're unsure of. What are they? Share them with us at #InnovateInsideTheBox or with a group of your peers/ colleagues.

3. How can you empower your students to build their powers of observation to identify resources that will help them meet their goals?

Please share to #InnovateInsideTheBox

Chapter 10
CREATORS

Students should be able to own
their learning by creating stuff
that matters to them.

—Chris Lehman and Zac Chase

Here is a little confession: I have a gigantic #ManCrush on Ryan Gosling. I think he is amazingly talented and love his range in so many roles; *La La Land* is in my top ten movies of all time! He is one of my favorite actors in the world and has been for a long time. And he is Canadian!

That is why I laughed hysterically when I saw a series on the Vine app (I miss you so much, Vine!) called "Ryan Gosling won't eat his cereal." In segments no longer than six seconds each, someone would find clips of Ryan Gosling in movies and try to feed him a spoonful of cereal by standing in front of a screen and slowly moving cereal to his mouth—that he would ultimately deny. It was amazing how many different ways Ryan Gosling would deny the cereal (he is so versatile), from making faces of disgust to actually making movements to swat the cereal away from his mouth. Every six-second video would bring me to tears as it was so random yet funny.

The mastermind behind the videos was Ryan McHenry, a Scottish film director. With each short creation, he brought joy to the world and smiles to a ton of people. Ryan Gosling even acknowledged in an April 2015 tweet that one thing people didn't know about him was that he actually loved cereal, a little nod to the meme created by Ryan McHenry.

In 2013, Ryan McHenry was diagnosed with a form of cancer, osteosarcoma. Through his diagnosis, chemotherapy treatments, and remission, he continued to make short videos that connected a community to his story. The cancer eventually returned, and McHenry passed away in May of 2015.[1] I didn't even know about McHenry's passing until I saw a strange video of a bowl of cereal on Vine, with Ryan Gosling taking a spoonful of cereal, making a slight nod, and eating cereal in front of the audience. Gosling actually created a Vine account just to take a moment to eat cereal and acknowledge McHenry.[2] Gosling then followed up with a tweet: "My heart goes out to all of Ryan McHenry's family and friends. Feel very lucky to have been a part of his life in some small way."[3]

Seriously, Ryan Gosling? You have to be gorgeous, talented, *and* sweet?

I share this story of Ryan McHenry and Ryan Gosling often as something that seems so ridiculous and minute, but actually has a very powerful underlying message. Little creations that may seem insignificant can have a big impact on the world. In education, we talk about developing the next person to create "Facebook," but the little cereal videos McHenry created brought smiles to so many people in a time when it seems we need more light in the world.

When my daughter was born, I played a song titled "Growing Up" by Ryan Macklemore on repeat. My favorite lines from the song are . . .

> *Don't try to change the world, find something that you love*
>
> *And do it every day*
>
> *Do that for the rest of your life*
>
> *And eventually, the world will change*

What McHenry shared in his short twenty-seven years embodied this lyric to a tee. What we create doesn't have to be "big" to have an impact. Small gifts continuously shared over time can make an incredible difference in the world.

Why the Word Create Is So Crucial to Education in Our World Today

A quote from Thomas Friedman has shaped a lot of my thinking: "The world only cares about—and pays off on—what you can do with what you know (and it doesn't care how you learned it)."[5] In other words, it isn't what we know that matters; it is what we do with what we know—what we create—that matters. I believe that to be true, and yet I remember reading a Wikipedia article on "Internet Culture" that said only 1 percent of people online create content, and 99 percent consume.[6] I have no idea the validity of that statistic, but let's think of it in terms of school. How often do high school students in school consume information from Wikipedia versus contribute to a Wikipedia article, in a serious manner? Even in classrooms, we confuse *regurgitation of information* with *creation*. Chris Lehman, the CEO of the Science Leadership Academy Schools in Philadelphia, makes this point brilliantly: "If you assign a project and get back thirty of the exact same thing, that's not a project—that's a recipe."[7]

Are our students clamoring to "create" in schools? Maybe in kindergarten. But too often the need to create gets "schooled" out of them before they leave elementary school. I have worked with students in schools where their own mobile devices are not allowed in classrooms, and I ask them, "If you could bring your device, how would you use it in the classroom?" The typical answers I hear over and over again are "to Google stuff" and "as a calculator." It's always disheartening, because I know there is so much students can create with technology! Information searches and calculations don't even scratch the surface of what they could do with even a device as simple as their smartphone. But when they aren't encouraged to create or to explore the possibilities for creation, "to Google stuff" and "as a calculator" are the best they can come up with—at school. The story might be completely different at home.

Exploring the possibilities for creation is important for students—and for educators—particularly as it relates to technology. If you get a new set of tablets for the classroom, you may be inclined (like so many teachers are) to ask, "What apps should we download?" My encouragement is to ask first, "What can we create with these devices that we couldn't before?" A plane is not transformational if we only use it to drive from point A to point B; it is only transformational when we use the plane to fly. In the same way, technology is just a tool. If you don't choose to use it in transformational ways, nothing changes.

> **Technology is just a tool. If you don't choose to use it in transformational ways, nothing changes.**

The Importance of Meaningful Creation

It's important to note that creation and consumption are complementary ideas, not opposites. As John Spencer states, "It's easy to pit creativity and consumption against each other. However, critical consuming is vital for creative work. When you engage in critical consuming, you become more inspired and, ultimately, you will create better content."[8]

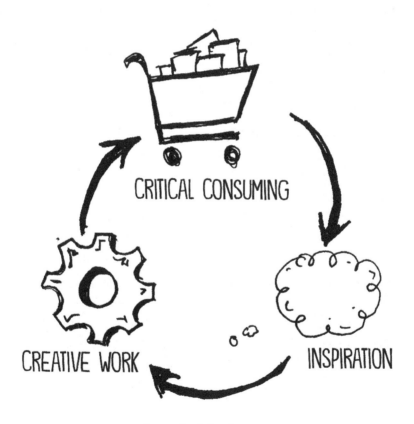

Image by John Spencer

But if critical consumption is important, we have to consider meaningful creation; when I say "meaningful," I mean that it is meaningful to the student, not only the teacher. For example, do you remember doing haikus in school? How often do you use them today? Might be a lot if you are a poet, but I can't say that this is the norm in my day-to-day (or even year-to-year) life. I saw an image of supposed student work and here was their Haiku:

> **Five syllables here.**
> **Seven more syllables there.**
> **Are you happy now?**

Actually meets the criteria but not necessarily meaningful to the student, right?

(When I wrote this, Katie sent me a note on the above sentence: "As a former ELA teacher, I have to tell you that, technically, a haiku needs to be about nature, so this doesn't meet the criteria." Thanks, Katie . . . insert Debbie Downer GIF.)

The second point in reference to meaningful creation is that it should have some academic value and be at the higher-order-thinking level beyond recall and knowledge, which requires taking what you consume and making something that did not previously exist. The critical distinction here is that if you just consume information and repackage it in diorama, slide presentation, or even a website, the expression of that information is not necessarily cognitively demanding—and may actually waste time instead of providing rich, meaningful learning experiences. This is where the higher order thinking skills and deep learning come into play, creating something new and better. Jennifer Gonzales notes in her post titled "Is That Higher Order Task Really Higher Order?" that "work at the create level doesn't really need glue, markers, scissors, or technology to qualify as a 'create' task. If you remove all the 'creative' trappings and just look at the mental work students are doing, it should still involve creating something new with the content they're learning."[8]

We need to clarify the goals and the view of *creation* to include an expanded view of what this means and ensure it is relevant to the task and the learner; for example, I am not necessarily in the "every kid should code" camp. I do believe that every student should have the opportunity to learn to code and have access and exposure in schools, as there are many benefits to learning to code. But just as I know there are benefits to playing basketball but don't believe every student should be forced to play, coding shouldn't be a requirement. "Makerspaces" are becoming more common in schools, which is great, but they are not the only place or way that students should have opportunities to create. We have to decide which things are necessary for all students (such as numeracy and literacy) and which things deserve exposure, opening doors for students to create things meaningful to them and challenging them to grow their knowledge, skills, and dispositions. When we discuss the need for personalization of education but then try to create standardized outcomes for all students, the notion of personalization becomes moot.

Writing this book right now, for example, is meaningful creation to me. The concepts I am wrestling with and trying to communicate are making me really think about what I know and believe. It is a mental exercise that requires a 360-degree view of what I am saying. I am

> **When we discuss the need for personalization of education but then try to create standardized outcomes for all students, the notion of personalization becomes moot.**

always thinking, "What is going to be the argument against what I am writing now, and how can I address it before it is brought to me?" Through this type of creation, you can see the characteristic of empathy as I am trying to understand the perspective of others, which I wouldn't necessarily need if I were only consuming information rather than putting it out in the world for others to consume.

Creation can be in the sciences, as well as in humanities, arts, athletics, technology, and many other avenues that are beneficial to a learner. We have to expand our view of creation so our students see themselves in the picture. When people understand creation from the perspective of doing it themselves, they have a better understanding of the work that is put into the process. I have always said that if I had to choose one, I would rather be a creator than a critic. Becoming a creator takes vulnerability but, as Brené Brown states, "Courage starts with showing up and letting ourselves be seen." [9]

Embracing Student-Centric Creations

In Universal Design for Learning, we want all students to be creators and makers. I asked my second-grade daughter what she wants to learn to make in school. Her answer? "I want to learn how to make robot puppies." Now, how many classes are providing her with the skills to make those robot puppies?! In all seriousness, our kids have passions and interests, and when we align our goals and standards with personalized assessments, magic happens. Assessments need to move beyond worksheets, essays, and presentations to more authentic applications that include student-centric creations.

Provide Multiple Means of Engagement

We are much more likely to persevere when we know our goal and are empowered to choose what we create to reach it. One of the UDL guidelines reminds educators to "optimize choice and autonomy."

- **Provide choices**. *Options* and *choices* are often used interchangeably, but they are not always synonymous. Too often, teachers give students options, but they do not give them choices. Students know what their options are. They know they can write blogs, produce videos, create projects, or work alone or with peers, but often they don't have a choice in what they create. After you have your *why*, consider taking the time to tell students, "This is what you'll be learning about in the next week. That is non-negotiable, but you get to decide what you want to create to show me that you met your goal. Let's list four possible options together, so you can make a choice about how to best meet your goals." (Innovate inside the box!) In a sixth-grade science class taught by the brilliant Caitlyn Morris, students had the following choices to express their understanding of the similarities and differences between solar and lunar eclipses:
  - Create a poster (use any art medium you wish or graphically design on your Chromebook)
  - Create a sketchnote (by hand or on Google Draw)
  - Create a slideshow
  - Create a Flipgrid video demonstration, and the link will be posted on Google Classroom (this could also be in homage to the Ryan Gosling cereal videos!)

As George noted above, I don't write a lot of haikus. But I frequently attend conferences and poster sessions, take notes, see my peers slay sketchnotes, and create slide decks and video clips weekly for presentations to convey my ideas and communicate with others. These creations are authentic and meaningful.

- **Understand the Paradox of Choice and the Rule of 5**. Choice is critical to build expert learning and an innovator's mindset, but too much choice can do the opposite. In his famous TED Talk, Barry Schwartz discusses how too many choices can result in paralysis and regret[10] (i.e., "I don't know which one to pick," and "Awwww, I wish I had picked the other one."). Research on hundreds of adults choosing retirement plans shows us that once you get over a "handful" of choices, people get antsy and stress spikes.[11] If you get over ten choices, paralysis sets in. So it seems that the magic number is five.

- **Identify the barriers first**. In the example above, Morris nails it with four choices to assess whether students understand the similarities and differences between solar and lunar eclipses. How do UDL practitioners create choices? They start by identifying the barriers. If, for example, Morris measures eclipse knowledge on a standardized test, some students may face barriers because they struggle with long-term retrieval or test anxiety. If she assigns an essay, some students may struggle with writing (granted, there are times when writing is necessary, like when your *goal* is actually writing). To eliminate these barriers, she provides four choices. If she gave them a list of eighty possible creations, she could probably kiss a class period goodbye (Hello, paralysis!). Identify the barriers, consider authentic products, and collaborate with students to create a short list (five or less) of products that allow all students to meet the goal.

Provide Multiple Means of Representation

If we want students to be creators and expert learners, they have to understand the concept of creativity. *Representation* in UDL requires educators to promote understanding of language through robust vocabulary development. The following options can help to teach students about creativity so they can become creators.

- **Define creativity**. Research is clear that creativity is a teachable phenomenon.[12] We need to promote an understanding of what it means to be creative by being transparent with students about how to develop it. The four most common methods to build creativity? Literally all of them align to the Innovator's Mindset. (I'm suddenly having visions of *Wayne's World* and Dana Carvey and Mike Myers bowing down and repeating, "We're not worthy." Looks like George nailed it.) The four ways to build creativity as outlined in the research are as follows:
  1. Collaborative projects ("Networked")
  2. Presenting and discussing exemplars of creativity ("Observant")
  3. Challenging students to find new solutions to existing problems ("Problem Finders/Solutions")
  4. Encouraging students to present their ideas using nonstandard formats, e.g., video, poetry, etc. . . . ("Creators")

Provide Multiple Means of Action and Expression

The section that follows provides hints, tips, and everyday wisdom for taking action on the fabulous four methods just discussed in order to build creativity.

- **Collaborative Projects**: Encourage students to work collaboratively, either in person or online. Empower them to network with classmates or extend their network to collaborate with students in "sister classrooms," which can be other classrooms in the school or across the world.

- **"Google" Your Classroom**: In your classroom, set up the space so students can flexibly work in small groups or stations. The Google office is designed for creativity, and your space needs to be the same way. Don't feel like you have to redesign yourself, as George stated in the example at the beginning of the chapter. Have the kiddos collaborate to redesign the space!

- **Present and Discuss Exemplars of Creativity**: If you do a Google search for "infomercial," you will find a treasure trove of examples of creativity. You'll find the same by watching *SharkTank*. Share the best examples you can find before you challenge students to create their own product. Sometimes, the most ridiculous ideas can be the best ones. One of my third-grade teachers, Jill Pierantozzi, brought in every board game she could get her hands on and encouraged students to research more online. Then, they were tasked to create an original game that helped them to develop an understanding of fractions. It was genius! Developing and playing board games allowed students to demonstrate and use their knowledge (YAY!) to create something meaningful. And because they developed these skills and were able to apply them, they also were able to demonstrate their knowledge and proficiency on a traditional assessment too.

- **Challenge Students to Find New Solutions**: One of my favorite walk-throughs in my district was in a high school engineering class. Students watched a video clip of an inventor pitching, and getting feedback, on a new product to investors - a container designed to make it easier for small children to pour things like juice or milk without spilling. Sadly, the inventor didn't land the deal, but my colleague, Mark Rocheleau, challenged students to pair up and further redesign the product. They were given fifteen minutes to use any resources available to address design flaws based on the feedback and marketing research results the inventor provided. The winner? The Liq-Suc (pronounced "lick suck" for marketing). Catchy, huh? Essentially, they created a mechanism that would suction the liquid out of the bottom of the jug and re-route it to the spout. Imagine starting every class with a problem like that or empowering students to bring in their own problems and work on the solution together.

- **Create Using Nonstandard Formats**: As I walk through classrooms in my district, I am blown away by how often our students are empowered to create. I have witnessed a sock puppet show to explain the outcomes of the Opium War in a history class (They pulled it off!), eaten at an authentic Colombian "restaurant" in a Spanish class, observed fourth-grade students creating a digital breakout for their teachers, and watched high school students compete in March Madness bracketed math assessments they created. As a teacher, you can offer engaging choices for assignments: art exhibits with written rationales, podcasts, simulations, mock interviews, poetry slams, blogs, skits or one-act plays, lab reports, presentations, debates, etc.

Moving Forward

Innovators need to be creators, not just consumers. With that in mind, teachers need to provide numerous opportunities for students to create by providing options and choices for students to collaborate, examine exemplars of creativity, find solutions to problems, use non-traditional formats to consume new information and content, and have the flexibility to put the ideas together to create and express new and better ideas.

Questions for Discussion

1. How can you adapt an upcoming assessment into an opportunity for students to create an authentic product? Remember to provide approximately five choices to inspire them.

2. How can you help students to comprehend that creativity can be learned by teaching them four strategies for building creativity?

3. How will you take action and promote creativity in your classroom using multiple means of action and expression?

Please share to #InnovateInsideTheBox

Chapter 11
RESILIENT

*I always did something I was a little not ready
to do. I think that's how you grow. When there's
that moment of "Wow, I'm not really sure I can
do this," and you push through those moments,
that's when you have a breakthrough.*

–Marissa Mayer

Actor/comedian Jim Carrey shared during a commencement speech about how his father inspired his dreams to become a comedian. His story takes a sharp turn because it reminds us that "sticking with something" might actually be the easiest thing to do, but not necessarily the right thing to do:

> *My father could have been a great comedian, but he
> didn't believe that that was possible for him, and so
> he made a conservative choice. Instead, he got a safe
> job as an accountant, and when I was twelve years
> old, he was let go from that safe job, and our family*

*had to do whatever we could to survive. I learned many great lessons from my father. Not the least of which was that **you can fail at what you don't want. So you might as well take a chance on doing what you love.**[1]*

The message here is powerful. You might fail either way—at something you want or something you don't want—so you might as well go for what you really want. This could be the same as "keep trying, never giving up on what you want." The term *resiliency* is often used in the context of "never giving up." That may be one facet of resiliency, but being resilient doesn't mean running into a brick wall over and over again, hoping one day you will get a different result. Being resilient means that you are persistent and work towards your goals which, at times, demands that you need to recognize when something isn't working, reevaluate, and try something new.

Sometimes resilience means learning from our struggles and finding a pathway to deeper meaning and purpose, whether it is in learning, work, or life. Think of this notion in a personal context; have you ever stayed in a relationship way too long that you knew wasn't working and never would? Sometimes, staying in situations is not necessarily about resilience and finding a way to make things work; it is more about comfort. As educators, we do this when we continue to stick with a strategy or resource because we have always used it, not because it is the best for the students we serve.

Bouncing Forward

Donna Volpitta, EdD, founder of the Center for Resilient Leadership, shares a more modern understanding of the term *resilience*, noting that it is less about enduring and more about finding a pathway forward:

Today, resilience has a much broader meaning. For researchers and professionals working with kids, it's not just about "bouncing back." It's about "bouncing forward." Resilience doesn't just mean getting back to normal after facing a difficult situation. It means learning from the process in order to become stronger and better at tackling the next challenge.[2]

In Jim Carrey's case, he learned from his own father's struggles and created a new pathway for himself. His journey wasn't always easy, but he was passionate about his direction. The same will be true for you and for your students; resiliency is much easier to tap into when you are passionate about your pursuit.

Why Are We Promoting Failure?

Some people seem to believe that promoting failure is synonymous with teaching resilience. As a school principal, I foresaw a communications nightmare when education started focusing on the importance of "failure" for our students. I understood the intent of the messaging from many educators, but how things are meant and how they are heard are sometimes very different. A.J. Juliani makes a nice distinction between the notion of *failure* and *failing*,[3] the former being final, and the latter being an active and ongoing practice. When you hear those who are deemed successful talking about the importance of failure, they often forget to share the most important part of the story—the part where they got back up and moved forward from the process. This is a crucial element to embody as educators to relate to our students to help ~~instill~~ nurture and grow the trait of resilience in our students.

I intentionally chose the phrase "nurture and grow" in the above paragraph instead of using the word "instill" because it is a trait many of our students already have. So many show tremendous resiliency simply by showing up to school each day as they deal with situations and circumstances that many adults, myself included, might not be able to handle. Some struggle and some excel despite tough situations, which is why, as was mentioned in Chapter 5, empathy is crucial in all situations to best serve our students. Even as we promote the importance of resiliency, let's be sure to honor and recognize those who embody this trait in abundance.

As we're thinking about how to nurture and grow resilience in our students, let's also rethink the things we do that have a detrimental effect on this essential trait. One of the common practices that can negatively impact resilience is the traditional award ceremony. The ceremonies can be harmful to the student who never receives awards, as well as to the one who loses rank. There are two situations where recognition is often given and where it is often ignored. Imagine you have two students, one from a home that is well off with both parents there to offer support, and the other from a single-parent family where the parent has to work considerable hours to make ends meet. Although both families love their children with all of their hearts, one child has a greater advantage financially and socially. This first child is not really engaged in academics and does not work as hard, but is able to easily meet all the rubric requirements for the year. The other child works diligently the entire year, with little support at home, and is barely able to pull off a 70 percent average. To whom would you give the achievement award?

This is important to note. We can easily make judgments on our students based on outside perceptions. We should never assume that a child who "has it all" *must* be doing well and a student who may have family struggles is destined for a certain type of life. In *all* situations, we need to recognize our students as individuals and do our best to bring out the best in them and create opportunities to develop resilience. As Sheryl Sandberg states in her book, *Option B: Facing Adversity, Building Resilience, and Finding Joy,* no one's life is perfect:

> I don't know anyone who has been handed only roses. We all encounter hardships. Some we see coming; others take us by surprise. It can be as tragic as the sudden death of a child, as heartbreaking as a relationship that unravels, or as disappointing as a dream that goes unfulfilled. The question is: When these things happen, what do we do next?[4]

Good and bad things have happened in my life. I'm sure the same is true for you. Learning to deal with and grow from difficult experiences equips us to be better able to handle tough situations so we can thrive regardless of what life throws our way. That is the gift we need to nurture within our students.

Showing Resilience in Serving Others

Resiliency is sometimes displayed in what we do when tough situations happen to others. Phillip Sossou, a senior in 2016 at Boston Latin School, showed resolve and dedication to making his school a more inclusive and better space after the community had received

Learning to deal with and grow from difficult experiences equips us to be better able to handle tough situations so we can thrive regardless of what life throws our way.

"negative press in response to allegations of racism."[5] Over a four-month period, Sossou took time to draw a portrait of all 411 seniors in the class with the intention of showing their uniqueness and creating a more inclusive environment for the entire community. Imagine the overwhelming emotion of students when they walked into school one day and saw portraits of themselves and each of their classmates, realizing this was all done by one person who was trying to bring the community together. If you remember in Chapter 5, former student Natalie Hampton shared that it only takes one person to change the world, and Sossou decided to be that one person for his school.

When he was interviewed by the *Boston Globe*, Sossou explained why he put in the time and effort to create something good when it would have been so easy to do something negative or simply ignore a tough situation: "I was trying to show everyone in a positive light. Our class has been kind of divided. Having these pictures helps us to embrace our diversity."

Resiliency is sometimes bringing people together when it would be much easier to push them apart. There are so many things we can learn from students all over the world, students like Sossou, if we are willing to see all the good they bring to the lives of others.

How Do We Develop Resiliency in Our Students?

I recently made an epic mistake. I booked a flight from Boston to Sacramento, so I could arrive bright and early to present in Pleasant Valley, California. At 1:15 a.m. Pacific, when I arrived at my hotel in Pleasant Valley, my body was on the struggle bus of 4:15 a.m. Eastern. Half asleep, I plugged in the address of the presentation venue on Waze so I knew what time to set my alarm.

The venue was 5 hours and 45 minutes from the hotel. Clearly, I typed it in wrong, right? Turns out, there is a Pleasant Valley School District in Ventura, California, and a Pleasant Valley, California. They are six hours away from each other, and I was in the wrong one and working on fumes. If I had a paper bag in my carry-on luggage, I would have been breathing into it.

Try to bottle that feeling for a moment. Anger, frustration, and embarrassment all wrapped up with a bow. Add in a healthy dose of exhaustion, and you have the potential for a meltdown. Do you scream? Cry? Punch something? Or do you buck up and solve the problem? I needed to change my environment, create a strategy, and bounce forward. I downloaded a book on Audible (shout out to *There, There* by Tommy Orange), opened the windows to catch a warm breeze, rolled in to a gas station to grab a seltzer, and hit the road.

Being able to sustain effort, persistence, and self-regulation *despite* that feeling is the key to resilience. I was able to do it because I have learned how. Someone taught me. Our task is to help all learners become purposeful and motivated, yet sometimes students face barriers that prevent them from sustaining effort and persistence and demonstrating self-regulation. We know the barriers that our students face: apathy, anxiety, trauma, disregulation, and the list goes on. The magic sauce is that regardless of these barriers, we can teach them to work through challenges by implementing the principles of UDL. By providing multiple means of engagement, representation, and action and expression, we can help to inspire our students, teach them the skills necessary to be resilient, and provide them with opportunities to show that they can, in fact, swallow an epic mistake like flying into the wrong Pleasant Valley—and be okay with "showering" in a Starbucks bathroom sink before walking into a keynote on zero sleep.

Here's the thing. When I walked into that presentation at 8:03 a.m. for an 8:30 a.m. presentation, I felt like Lady Gaga. I had traveled on the "tour bus" (aka my rental car) all night to be greeted by a room full of raving fans (or at least a room full of amazing teachers who were bright and ready to learn). Even though, ironically, failing is what ultimately led to that feeling of success. How can UDL prepare students to react with resilience in scenarios like this?

Provide Multiple Means of Engagement

UDL reminds us to examine our learning environment to minimize threats and distractions that prevent students from, as my seventh-grade students used to say, "getting their grit on." ("Novak, is it cool if I throw on my headphones? I need to get my grit on.")

- **Make it a place to be.** When I decided there was no other option than driving six hours overnight, I had to change my environment so I didn't explode like a pressure cooker. I'm sure you have your own sweet spot for your best work. I'd bet you a latte that it's not a sterile, white classroom with fluorescent lights and pods of desks. Work with students to give your learning environment a motivation makeover, so it's a place they can persevere. Ask them, "How could we redesign this room so we can focus, take risks, and work our tails off?" Based on their answers, bring in warm lighting, throw rugs, hooks for backpacks, plants, a bowl of mints, a diffuser for lavender, and multiple options for seating, such as yoga balls, a couch, etc. Encourage students to listen to music on earbuds, chew gum, and get cozy so they can "get their grit on." And always provide options for reflection. The magic of choice is having the ability to examine whether or not the choice fostered learning. An amazing exit ticket is the question,

"What options did you select to build your learning environment today, and how did it help you learn? Provide evidence of your learning!" Don't stop there! Empower students to vary the pace of work, length of work sessions, availability of breaks or time-outs, and the sequence of activities. Remember the key is providing flexible options so all students can choose the environment they need and reflect on how that environment increased their learning outcomes.

Please note: As much as the space is important for our students, we are firm believers the money for this should *not* be coming out of a teacher's pocket. Look at opportunities to create things within the constraints of what you have or innovate inside the box and perhaps have students connect with local groups to see what options are there (such as Craigslist for free furniture, donations from businesses, etc.). If students have the opportunity to find ways to build the classroom, they will feel a sense of ownership about the space they helped create.

- **Start with the *why*.** Simon Sinek, a leadership expert, popularized the phrase "Start with *why*." He argues that everyone has a *why*. Too often, our students don't feel motivated because lessons and assessments are not grounded in their *why*. We may state the goal or write it on the board, but inevitably some students' eyes may still look glazed like donuts. Don't torture yourself or your students this way! At the beginning of every lesson or project, ask students to come up with the most creative reasons why achieving the goal or standard could be important to them and empower them to identify a personal goal for reaching it. I once walked into a high school physical education class where the teacher asked students to come up with the most compelling reasons why it was important to demonstrate the mechanics of an overhand throw. The list included such critically important tasks that spanned from winning your "bae" a stuffed animal at the carnival to having to catch and release a hand grenade. Have them collaborate to create charts, infomercials, a bulletin board, etc., with visuals, vision boards, or motivational quotes as a visual representation of how important the work is. Relate back to this work every time they experience setbacks.

- **Embrace mistakes**. Literally. Sara Blakely, the billionaire founder of Spanx (you know, the slimming undergarments) provides bonuses and awards for employees who make the best mistakes each cycle. She also publicly shares her "favorite mistakes."[6] Why? Because failing means that you tried, and you took a risk. Consider the same in your classroom. What if we could help students to see failing as an opportunity to celebrate? What if you gave students the option to share what they learned from failing? Could you create a "Bouncing Forward" bulletin board or blare Britney Spears "Oops I Did It Again" from your computer? These practices minimize the threat of failing and allow students to understand that motivation is sometimes laced with a healthy dose of "suck."

Provide Multiple Means of Representation

When faced with a meaningful goal and the inevitable challenges that come with something out of reach, we have to rely not only on motivation, but the ability to cope. I am sure Edison really wanted to invent the lightbulb, but after the nine hundredth failure, I can imagine the poor guy needed a yoga class. As much as I wanted to get to the correct Pleasant Valley, I had to swallow the urge to scream profanities while laying on the horn.

Just like academic skills, we have to teach students how to self-regulate. No one means of representation will work for everyone. So flexibility and innovation are key.

- **Activate background knowledge**. We can't just expect kids to self-regulate and "bounce forward." We have to teach them to cope when faced with challenges and mistakes. Prerequisite skills like the ability to pause, breathe deeply, and be mindful, for example, may need to be pre-taught through demonstration and practice. Apps like GoNoodle and Calm, for example, are great to provide students with this modeling. Additionally, when we teach students about locus of control, it allows them to let go of things out of their control (the weather cancelled their soccer game) while focusing on things they can fix (they were a poor sport and the coach had them sit out until they could be a team player).
- **Embrace Exemplars**. Use multiple examples and non-examples when teaching coping strategies. Although cursing and hitting a wall may feel really cathartic, those reactions are "non-examples" of effective coping strategies. Be clear and transparent about teaching them to identify their emotions, encourage them to share what they know about coping, and how they currently try to cope, and as the brilliant educator you are, help them to connect their understanding to new, more effective learning.

Provide Multiple Means of Action and Expression

Action and expression require strategy and practice (and failing). Success is not just a one-and-done, not even in the real world. (How many of us had to retake our SAT? Teacher license exam?) The following classroom practices don't just tell students to keep trying, they provide them with opportunities to put effort into action so they can experience that success really just means you stuck with something longer than everyone who quit.

- **Allow revisions and retakes**. I've heard it before. *They "should" study the first time. They "should" not be given another chance. It's not fair for students who got it the first time.* Yep, I've heard it all, but if you're going to tell students not to give up, then don't prevent them from actually practicing resilience. Also, for the love of all that is good, when you do encourage revisions and retakes, give them the updated grade. You don't need to average the grades together and punish a student for a first attempt. They persevered and learned. Allowing them to experience that success will stay with them. To put things in perspective, if you fail your driver test, do they average the scores? NO! They take the second attempt as an isolated incident because they really hope you have improved for your safety and the safety of others.

- **Provide scaffolds**. Some students will fall, and they will feel like they can't go on. Our job is to provide them with supports to keep them moving in the right direction. These scaffolds may include exemplars, graphic organizers, word banks, peer-review opportunities, feedback, checklists, etc. Now, you may argue, *But we can't possibly provide those on assessments or revisions. That's not fair. That's not real life.* Oh, but it is. I bet more than half of you reading this are wearing contacts or glasses. Vision is kind of important when you're driving. Imagine you failed a vision test and your license was revoked because you couldn't wear your glasses. Would that make you want to keep trying to take that test, or would that, by definition, be the real injustice and make you want to put your fist through a wall? If we want students to continue to work independently toward their goals, we need to give them the tools to do that.

- **Model resilience**. To provide options for expression, we have to provide options for support. One oldie but goodie is the importance of modeling and sharing our strategies for improving our craft. Nothing says "I believe in continuous improvement" like ending every class with, "If I could do one thing differently tomorrow to improve your learning, what would it be?" To prompt students, provide them with a great sentence starter, such as "It would be cool if ___," and then truly listen. Embrace how you need to try again and do things differently, sharing after the fact your strategies for recognizing your failings and moving forward as a stronger teacher.

Moving Forward

Innovators need to build resilience as setbacks and failing are expected. "Failure" and "failing" are different. Whereas failure is final, *failing* happens as part of an ongoing practice of trying and learning. It's a practice that we can foster in our classrooms by implementing the principles of UDL. We want our students to practice failing and self-regulating as they work toward success because resilience can be learned and optimized in our schools when we give students the opportunities and support they need.

Questions for Discussion

1. What concrete strategies can you implement in your learning environment as you provide multiple means of engagement to increase student motivation and help them to embrace their *why*?

2. How will you incorporate more discussions on the importance of failing and "bouncing forward" with students while activating their background knowledge of coping strategies?

3. Students need models of resilience, yet many adults don't acknowledge setbacks as opportunities for growth. How can encouraging student feedback about our teaching highlight our own struggles and help us to model resilience?

Please share to #InnovateInsideTheBox

Chapter 12
REFLECTION

*Sometimes, you have to look back
in order to understand the
things that lie ahead.*

–Yvonne Woon

Easily, one of my favorite *Seinfeld* episodes ever is when George Costanza is at a meeting, eating the free shrimp off the table as quickly as possible, when one gentleman makes the comment, "Hey, George, the ocean called. They're running out of shrimp!" George, with a mouthful of shrimp, is embarrassed and has no idea what to say. A few moments later, they show George Costanza driving in his car getting more and more upset about the moment, replaying it in his mind, and then suddenly he says, "Ohhh, *yes*! That's what I should have said!" In his ability to have time to process, he comes up with an idea to have the same insult hurled back at him, ready with a new response, "Oh yeah? Well, the jerk store called. They are running out of you!"

Okay, maybe this isn't the best example of why reflection matters. (I still love the story and have used the "jerk store" comment on my closest friends for years.) But there is a point to sharing this story. We've all had that experience where we don't know what to say at the moment because we haven't had time to process, and then we replay that moment over and over again in our heads, thinking about what our response could have been. (There is actually a meme term for this called an "afterism," defined as "a clever comeback you don't think of until it's too late.")

The ability to reflect is crucial for understanding and processing. It is also essential to our ability to move forward and create something from what we have learned.

Reflection Time Is Learning Time

Reflection time is something that should be seen as vital to learning in education. But is that how it is always treated? More often than not, in North America, reflection is too often seen as "nice to have" but not a necessity. Consider the following scenario:

You are at a professional learning conference and hear a fantastic opening keynote. It is full of powerful stories and learning that really pushes your thinking and gets to the sweet spot of making you feel uncomfortable while also validating a lot of your path. You are blown away by the information, and there is so much to digest and ponder. The keynote ends and you pick up your things and *rush* to your next session because you know it might be packed. You might have to go to the bathroom, but OMG the line is *sooooo* long, so you skip the bathroom and get to the session just in time. The presenter, who left the keynote early to set up, has no idea what you just learned, and the session takes your thoughts in a totally different direction. Within minutes, what you just picked up is now gone, and you have already changed gears into something new. Session after session continue like this with new stuff and no time. By the end of the day, you are exhausted. You go home and your partner says, "Hey! How was the conference? What did you learn today?" You mumble, "Nothing," lay on the couch, unable to think or move, and fall asleep watching Netflix.

Hopefully, the above scenario is not as prevalent in the world of education for adults as it once was, but it is still the norm. If you read the above paragraph and thought, *Wow, that is a super ineffective way to do a one-day learning conference,* imagine how high school students around the world feel cycling through that same process five days a week. We talk about "consumption and creation," but it should be "consumption, reflection, and creation"—and not necessarily always in that order.

I believe we, as educators, need a jolt to our own learning experiences before we start creating solutions for students. I remember the first time I went to Australia for a conference. Each presentation was followed by a thirty-minute tea break. When I saw the thirty-minute break between each session, I thought, *That is a LONG time to go to the bathroom and grab a drink.* A break like that between sessions was not something I was used to for professional learning days.

> We talk about "consumption and creation," but it should be "consumption, reflection, and creation"—and not necessarily always in that order.

What happened next was incredible. People started talking to one another about what they just learned. They made their own connections to the content. Some people went off by themselves and started writing about what they learned. *What was this insanity?!* That one experience forever changed me, but then I started thinking about how I—and many others I connected with at conferences— shared that the best learning time was often the conversations with colleagues in the hallways. The time for processing is so valuable. If you are planning a conference, don't plan "breaks"— call it "reflection and connection time" and give ample time to do just that. If a person needs a break, they will take it. What they might not take on their own is time to process. Here is the real point: We *all* need time to reflect on our learning. So let's start asking, "How do we create this reflection and connection time for our students?"

Inward Reflection Is Crucial to Growth and Development

According to Helen Immordino-Yang, a professor of education, psychology, and neuroscience at the University of Southern California, reflection and processing time is crucial to the development of our students.

> *We focus on the outside world in education and don't look much at inwardly focused reflective skills and attentions, but inward focus impacts the way we build memories, make meaning, and transfer that learning into new contexts. What are we doing in schools to support kids turning inward?*

> *Balance is needed between outward and inward attention, since time spent mind wandering, reflecting, and imagining may also improve the quality of outward attention that kids can sustain.*[1]

That "mind wandering," as referred to by Immordino-Yang, has often been seen as a negative, but as Will Willimon, a professor at Duke Divinity School in Durham, North Carolina, says, "Daydreaming can be the mind's incubator."[2] How many students on any given day are told to quit daydreaming? What if, as writer Sidney Stevens asks, this act can have many benefits, such as heightening the ability to perform complex mental tasks, boosting intelligence, increasing creativity, and helping with stress and relaxation?[3] How might we redirect or encourage mind-wandering as a means of reflection that helps learners process ideas and move forward on them?

Reflection Is a Process That Needs to Be Learned

I am a huge advocate for blogging. Because I know the impact it can have on learning, I schedule three writing times each week where I write something to share with the world. I can't tell you that my writing is always good, but taking time to write and think helps clear my mind and deepen my own learning. It also helps that I know anyone can read it. It makes me more thoughtful of what I share and different perspectives (empathy) when I know anyone can read what I put out there.

Even if you don't want to blog, consider making space in the day for reflection with these three simple questions:

1. What went well today?
2. Where do I need to grow?
3. What will I do to move forward to build on my strengths and weaknesses?

This simple process, referred to as "making meaning," by Arthur L. Costa and Bena Kallick, the founders of The Institute for the Habits of Mind, allows us to dig deep into our learning.[4]

Col. Eric Kail, the course director of military leadership at the US Military Academy at West Point, made this important connection to how reflection actually helps us to grow and look back to grow forward.

> *Reflection requires a type of introspection that goes beyond merely thinking, talking, or complaining about our experiences. It is an effort to understand how the events of our life shape the way in which we see the world, ourselves, and others . . . . Reflection is what links our performance to our potential.*[5]

> # Reflection is what links our performance to our potential.

Time alone, both in and out of school or work, is necessary to our development as individuals. I would almost say that the pendulum in education has over-shifted from isolation to collaboration, without understanding that many need their own time to connect within themselves. The ability to work with others is crucial, but we don't have to do it all of the time, especially when collaboration can take place in face-to-face or virtual environments. Human connection (face-to-face) is essential, but so is human disconnection. Finding ways for our students (and ourselves) to meaningfully reflect forward on their learning is vital to the work we do as learners and innovators. A great idea only matters when we have the ability to think it through and put it into action.

Learn to Choose, Choose to Learn

My auntie Jan once told me, "Guilt is a useless emotion." So often, we look back on mistakes we have made with regret and guilt as opposed to determining the source of what went wrong and fixing it. Costanza was beating himself up that he missed the "jerk store" comment instead of doing something more productive, like filling his colleagues' desk drawers with shrimp. (Nah, that would only result in more guilt!)

We attend professional development and get nothing out of it and then feel guilty that we took a day away from our students, for what? Subpar coffee and brownies during a five-minute break? Our students all fail a test, or misbehave for the sub, and we feel guilty. Listen to my auntie Jan: Guilt is *useless*.

It's okay, good even, to look back. Just make sure that you are practicing meaningful reflection, not self-loathing. Reflecting empowers you to move forward and take action instead of getting stuck in that cycle of regret or jumping into the hamster wheel of rushing forward and not even taking the time to look back.

This isn't just for us as educators. Opportunities for reflection are bursting at the seams in our schools. We have so many discipline initiatives in our schools that are focused on students taking the time to reflect on their decisions and the consequences of those decisions. Open circles, restorative justice, and responsive classroom are all frameworks and practices that address the problem of students not reflecting on their mistakes.

When we empower students to reflect on their actions and learning as a springboard toward future decision making, we make the connection to what it means to fail forward. But just as there is very little time taken in professional development for reflection, reflection time is often non-existent in our classrooms.

When implementing UDL, which requires student choice, reflection is a critical step. One teacher who is doing this well is Mike Anderson, the author of *Learning to Choose, Choosing to Learn*. When providing students with options and choices, Anderson uses a process he calls "choose, do, review."[6] It's a classic recipe to build executive function in students and foster effective decision-making and learning.

Step 1: Choose. Imagine one of the following scenarios. If you're an elementary teacher, imagine that you set up a menu of math tasks. You ask students to choose the ones that are most challenging for them, as well as any resources that would help them solve the problems. There is a table with manipulatives, white boards, sample problems, and iPads. If you teach middle or high school, you ask students to take fifteen minutes to activate or build background knowledge on the causes of the Civil War before you start the unit. You provide multiple options for students with the prompt, "Choose two of the following six resources to activate your background knowledge about the Civil War." You provide links to primary source documents, the online textbook, video documentaries, and a podcast from a professor. In both scenarios, you tell your students they can work alone or with a partner, and you trust them to choose what they feel works best.

Step 2: Do. Without much thought, if any, students feverishly make eye contact with their besties and dive into resources based on what seems the easiest, the most fun, etc. You know what happens next. Some partners are a hot mess and many students are distracted. Students who would benefit from scaffolds choose not to use them. Only one person in each group is doing the work. Now at this point, most people are ready to throw this UDL baloney out the window. This is when I hear the following: "But what if they choose the easier thing every time?" or "Students don't know how to make great choices," or "Whenever I do this, it turns out to be a disaster." I see you, and I believe you. But making great choices is a skill that every student can learn. They may have not learned it yet. Skills like note-taking, collaboration, and self-reflection need to be taught with as much passion as reading and writing. So here is my best advice to you. When you provide students with a goal and some choices, you will sit and observe. As a teacher this may be painful, but as they say in poker, "Let it ride."

Step 3: Review. You gave those little love birds a goal, and a task, and now is a great time to do a little formative assessment. Not for a grade, of course, but to help them determine how effective their choices were in meeting the goal. This is the power of choice—the reflection period. My students knew this was coming, and after the first time I did it, they were always ready for it. When they nailed the questions I asked in a Google Form, exit ticket, or class discussion, they were able to reflect and determine that their choices were effective. When they bombed it like a Bath Fizzers Unicorn Bath Soak, they knew it meant a chitty-chat about their choices. Every Friday we would host a little episode I called "Hooray! Hooray! It's Re-Do Day," and we would review our work from the week, reflect on our strengths and areas we needed to improve, and we would make better decisions. But here's the thing. It wasn't punitive in any way, shape, or form. These conferences were an opportunity for me to check in and ask them to share their goals, their strategies, what worked and what didn't, and why, and we would discuss how to make better decisions the next time. How often do your students have this opportunity?

Making choices starts and ends with the process of reflection. Being reflective means taking a very hard look inside yourself to determine why something happened and what you should do next. That really is the core of improvement. But so often, the review portion is swept under the rug. How often have we handed back essays and students have immediately thrown them in the recycling bin? Not anymore.

Multiple Means of Engagement

To optimize the importance of the "choose, do, review" cycle, we as educators have to provide opportunities for students to participate in meaningful review opportunities.

- **Highlight mistakes**. One fabulous strategy I love is to "correct" student work by highlighting mistakes but not grading them, similar to the "Delaying the Grade" strategy highlighted in Chapter 2 by Kristy Louden. I first learned about this strategy by viewing a *Teacher Channel* video featuring Leah Alcala, a seventh- and eighth-grade math teacher. She notes in the video, "I am highlighting where their mistake is, but I'm not mentioning specifically what that mistake is." She goes on to say, "So you really can't look at the number of highlights and determine your grade. It is a much more involved, nuanced process of understanding what types of mistakes this kid is making and how important are those mistakes in terms of learning math."[7] This process can be done on any assessment—think science labs, essays, and document-based questions. The very nature of the strategy requires students to reflect and continue learning after the assessment is "done."

- **Use exam wrappers:** Exam wrappers are short activities that direct students to review their performance on an assessment or project after it has been reviewed or graded by the teacher. It's not only a surefire way to avoid graded tests paper-airplaning themselves into the recycling bin, but it's a great opportunity to ask students to reflect on how well they prepared, the risks they took, the mistakes they made, and how well the design of instruction prepared them.

Multiple Means of Representation

Highlight the process of "choose-do-review" with students so they understand that it's a critical aspect of learning. Remember to provide multiple means of representation to ensure all students understand the process!

- **Teach Choose-Do-Review**. Make a bulletin or, better yet, empower students to design bumper stickers or temporary tattoos so they have received the message in multiple means. Many students simply think they are or are not good at something. The power of "choose-do-review" is that learning and improvement are processes. If students take the time to reflect, they have moved one inch closer to the goal the next time. As Al Pacino said in *Any Given Sunday*, "The inches we need are everywhere around us. On this team, we fight for that inch. On this team, we tear ourselves and everyone around us to pieces for that inch. We claw with our fingernails for that inch. Cause we know when we add up all those inches, that's going to make the difference." Too dramatic? I think not. (P.S. Even though this is pretty much the best sports pump-up clip of all time, there is a swear in it that may ruin it for inspiring your students.)

Multiple Means of Action and Expression

Providing opportunities for students to reflect in engaging ways, and teaching them the basics of reflection, is super important. But if we want them to embrace reflection in their daily lives, we have to be sure we teach them to be strategic and take action on their reflection.

- **Scaffold reflection**. Provide students with tools, so they can reflect on their learning through rubrics, checklists, and the results of diagnostic and formative assessments. Ultimately, the goal would be for students to use these resources as well as their teachers and peers to consistently reflect on their performance, ask for feedback, change their strategies, and revise their work to promote and highlight growth.

- **Self-reported grading**. Consider collaborating or empowering students to draft their own report card comments. This is an excellent opportunity for students to show that they understand their learning and are reflecting on what they need to improve and where their strengths lie.

Moving Forward

Taking time to reflect is critical for expert learning and innovation. Not only do students need time to make meaning of what they learned, but they also need to reflect on their strategies for learning and create goals for improvement. When implementing UDL, teachers provide students with choices in how they learn, what they learn, and how they share what they know, but for this to be effective, teachers have to embrace a process of "choose-do-review," which begins and ends with meaningful reflection.

Questions for Discussion

1. What do you feel guilty about as a teacher? Reflect on that and consider how to move forward. Make a plan!

2. Consider every class period a process of "choose-do-review." How will students be accountable for meaningful reflection?

3. In what types of assessments could you "highlight mistakes" to prompt student reflection?

Please share to #InnovateInsideTheBox

PART THREE

You Are the Change You Seek

In Part Two, we discussed how to foster an Innovator's Mindset in students using the principles of UDL. Essentially, we broke down how to instill eight characteristics using the three principles: Multiple means of engagement, representation, and action and expression, and hopefully it's clear that none of these are isolated. One cannot be empathetic without being observant and reflective. One cannot be a risk-taker without resilience. And one cannot be a creator without being a problem-finder or problem-solver who is networked. And to implement UDL, educators need to develop each of the eight characteristics in themselves first. All of the characteristics and principles weave themselves together in an intricate pattern that ultimately leads to empowered, expert learners. These learners have the tools they need to partner with educators to co-design learning through equitable and meaningful experiences. At the core of these experiences are the relationships that we build with our students.

Clearly, we haven't addressed all possible barriers in our education systems within these pages. What we *have* done is lay a foundation comprised of relationships, commitment to continuous learning, and an Innovator's Mindset that we can use to attack the more systemic barriers. This foundation, coupled with a commitment to your own continuous learning, allows for the deconstruction of practices and systems that don't work for learners. And that starts with the rejection of the "one-size-fits-all" approach to education.

In the book *Unlearning*, Alison Posey and Katie Novak discuss the differences between equality, equity, and expert learning. The visual below from the book depicts where we want all learners to be when they have both an Innovator's Mindset and a universally designed education: expert learning. It's an update on the old baseball equality vs. equity visual, where the kiddos look like they are stealing the game. We need a system that doesn't just allow them to see the game by looking over a fence, but one that gets them tickets to experience it, and to be a part of the magic. The classic "Take Me Out to the Ballgame" song explicitly says, "Take me out with the crowd," not, "Get me a box so I can peek over the fence and still be an outsider" (which clearly doesn't have the same rhythm). Expert learning builds upon the concept of equity by promoting empowerment and involvement, which is what the Innovator's Mindset is all about. Yes!

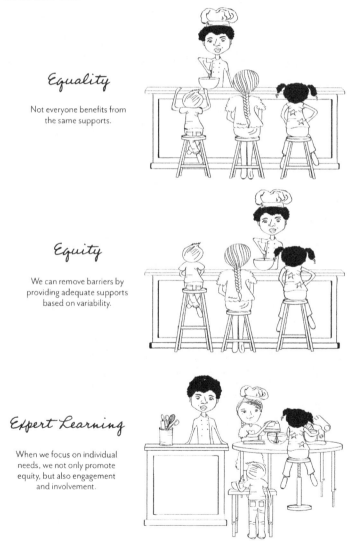

Equality

Not everyone benefits from the same supports.

Equity

We can remove barriers by providing adequate supports based on variability.

Expert Learning

When we focus on individual needs, we not only promote equity, but also engagement and involvement.

Consider this visual a transition because in the closing two chapters of this book, we will remind you how important *you* are, no matter your role on this journey. Before we get there, though, please pause to reflect on the questions asked at the beginning of this book:

1. What has challenged you?
2. What has been reaffirmed?
3. What will you do moving forward?

Hopefully, throughout this book you saw evidence of the first two questions, but the third question is the one that really matters. What action will come from you reading this book? This is where the shift happens in education. We can consume pages and hours' worth of great content, but until we do something with it, we have no ownership over the process of learning. We would love to hear your reflections at #InnovateInsideTheBox. What has changed in your practice? What have you made better? Your story matters. Share it.

In the final two chapters, we encourage you to think about two things. In Chapter 13, we want you to think about the influence you have on yourself and others. The whole reason we have asked you to "innovate inside the box" is that no matter when you pick up this book, or where you are, you are very likely facing challenges—as are your colleagues and students. You can have a major impact on your work and on the lives of those you serve when you implement what you've learned here. If, by your example and sharing, you influence one other teacher to change his or her practice, you will have made a difference in the lives of hundreds, if not thousands, of kids' lives.

In Chapter 14, we want to acknowledge and remind you how hard this work is in education. We value any person who has taken their own time to read this book, to better their practice. But we want to remind you how important *you* are to this process. We need you to take care of yourself, and we know how hard this career is that you have chosen. The shift in focus to the whole "child" is important in education, but we need to focus more on the "whole" educator.

The hope for this book is that this is the beginning of a dialogue not only with each other and colleagues, but a reminder on the importance of the dialogue we need to start having more with ourselves. Keep reading; what comes next is for *you.*

Chapter 13
LEAD FROM WHERE YOU ARE

If you look for problems, you will find problems; if you look for solutions, you will find solutions.

–Andy Gilbert

Throughout this book, Katie and I have provided ideas and strategies utilizing the characteristics of the Innovator's Mindset and the UDL principles. Our hope is that you will find them valuable enough to implement them in your practice, modifying them to best serve the learners in front of you. Hopefully, we've also inspired you to innovate ideas for yourself and co-create solutions with your learners and your unique circumstances. But I want to make sure you hear this from me too: I know that teaching is an insanely hard job. I do not expect you to *immediately* change *everything* you're doing because a) it is not feasible, and b) you were already doing great things before you read this book. Katie and I encourage you to share what you're doing, not only so we can see what you have learned but also so we can have the opportunity to learn from you. An educator with minimal years of experience has something they can share with the most veteran of educators, and obviously vice-versa. We can learn from anyone, if we are open to growth.

What I hope is that you look at *something* that you are currently doing and ask yourself, "Is there a better way?" If there isn't, then you are on the right path. But if there is, try just one thing in pursuit of providing something better for the learners you serve. One thing at a time, over time, can lead to massive change in a career and the impact on learners.

Change can be hard, but it is not impossible, and the right changes can move everything in a better direction. I can identify many moments in my life where one little thing completely altered my trajectory. Let me tell you about just one. Ever since I was a kid, I have loved basketball. I grew up loving the Lakers' Magic Johnson. I watched any basketball game that showed on Canadian television which, in a country obsessed with hockey, seemed like about five games a year. (P.S. . . . This has changed significantly in Canada, especially now that the Toronto Raptors have won the 2019 NBA Championship!) I played basketball in high school and knew that, one day, I wanted to be a coach.

My dream came true. In my first job, I became the senior boys basketball coach, and I wanted to be the best coach I could be. We had an awesome group of players, and I thought that with my coaching, I could make them better. Having been influenced by the coaches I saw watching the NBA, I will tell you, if I didn't like a call, I let the referees know. I would yell at the referees across the court, aware of just how much noise I could make to get their attention without crossing the "line" and earning a technical foul. As a coach, based on my NBA mentors, I saw complaining about calls as part of my job. That being said, I became frustrated when my players would complain to the referees about calls they would or wouldn't get. The boys didn't have the same awareness of the "line" that I did. They would mouth off, and the technical fouls they got as a result often cost our team. In my mind, I saw the yelling from my players as more about their immaturity and less about my example and my coaching.

This changed one day, a few months into my coaching career, when I was extremely frustrated with the lack of calls my team was getting. I was visibly upset with the referees and I called a time-out. Before I went to the huddle, one of the referees, who was also a teacher at another school, came over to me and said in a calm tone, "Hey, George, I know you love basketball, and I can tell you love these kids, and I can tell these kids love you. I just want you to know this: Whether you yell at us or not, your players look up to you and will do what you do. What example do you want to set?"

I never yelled at a referee again.

Not only did I not ever yell at a referee again, with this new lesson I focused more on what I could control which, first and foremost, was the example I was setting for my players. Referees still made some bad calls, but I realized yelling had little impact on what the referees would do—and a huge impact on what my players would do. So I focused on our game and my coaching, and those things changed the game for us and helped us become a better team.

I think about that interaction with that referee-teacher often. He had no idea whether his words mattered. I am sure as an experienced referee, that encounter was not his first with an overheated coach. But on that day, he changed everything for me. It was not only what he said, but how he said it and what he invoked in me. He started by acknowledging my value: "*I know you love basketball and I can tell you love these kids, and I can tell these kids love you.*"

That got my attention.

He also understood what drove me: I wanted my kids to excel, not only in basketball but in life. My own coach, Kevin Grieman, had a significant impact on me as a person, one that lasts with me to this day. I hoped to be that kind of influence for my players and my students. I wanted my coaching to be about something bigger than basketball. This still drives me in my work with educators and students. As hard as I try, I can tell you that there are still times I have failed since that interaction, but I do my best to wake up in the morning and help others each day.

One other thing of note: he gave me the choice to change my direction. He never thrust change upon me. He simply asked me a question to make me reflect on my influence: *"Your players look up to you and will do what you do. What example do you want to set?"*

The only way to help move people forward is through building relationships and understanding where their journey begins, not focusing solely on where you want them to be.

He knew that it is impossible to *make* people change. He could never have forced me to stop yelling. Even getting thrown out of the game would not have had the same impact as the words he offered calmly that night. He created the conditions that ensured change would be more likely. That's all any of us can do. That single, fifteen-second interaction was a master class in helping me embrace a better way forward. The only way to help move people forward is through building relationships and understanding where their journey begins, not focusing solely on where you want them to be.

What Stands in Your Way?

Here is another point to the story above that is extremely important. The person who made that comment was a peer. He was not my boss, not my administrator, not my superintendent, and not some government official. He was a colleague. It is a reminder that we shouldn't take this lightly: *It does not matter what your position is; you can influence change. If education is going to move forward, you can't wait for "someone else" to do it.* You have a bigger influence on changing the "system" than you give yourself credit for—especially if you are a teacher. Do you know who teachers tend to listen to when it comes to changing practice in their classroom? Other teachers. We can't say, "Who am I to make a difference with my colleagues?" and then complain when a politician wants to change something in our schools and say, "What do they know?! They have never taught in a school." You, whatever your position, can have an incredible amount of influence on your peers.

> It does not matter what your position is; you can influence change. If education is going to move forward, you can't wait for "someone else" to do it.

Just like you can learn from whomever you are open to learning from, you can influence people, no matter how they are connected to you on the traditional "hierarchy" in your organization. This means that, although there is much to learn for new teachers, they can also have wisdom and ideas that can impact an experienced teacher who has been teaching for twenty years. If we are open to learning with and from others, we will realize and value the wisdom that exists in all of our schools. We have to start elevating those within our own organizations. The experts in education might be on the other side of the world, but they are for sure down the hallway. We need to tap into one another.

So how do we make this change happen in our own communities, no matter our position? Below are some effective practices, in any position, to lead and help others not only accept change, but embrace it as an opportunity to do something better for kids.

1. **Bring it back to the kids.** Whenever I hear someone sharing a shift in practice, one question always comes to mind: How does this benefit students? This question needs to stay at the forefront of all decisions made in education. As one teacher told me, "Educators are not scared of change. They are scared of wasting their time on something that has no benefit to students." Educators, no matter their role, do not simply have full plates but full platters, and they are overflowing. If you can't clearly articulate the benefit to learners, then the "change" is probably not necessary. Always ask when considering a new change for implementation: Am I adding to the person or adding to the plate?

2. **Model the change you want to see.** Although this might seem extremely cliché, it is the most imperative step for leading any change effort. It is common to talk about the idea that people need to be "risk-takers," yet, too often, we are not willing to model taking risks ourselves. True leaders, whatever their position, lead by example. Until people see change modeled, they will not feel comfortable doing something new themselves.

There is a powerful difference between talking from a "theoretical" view and speaking from "practice" in terms of the credibility and influence you can have with those you serve. Have you ever seen a slide presentation on "21st Century Change" from an administrator who does not exhibit any of the learning that is being discussed in the presentation? Me too. Those presentations rarely result in the desired change. Instead, people will feel more comfortable taking a journey to an unknown place if they know the first steps have been taken by someone else. Chris Kennedy, superintendent in West Vancouver, Canada, shares that educators need to be "elbow deep in learning" with others, not only to show they are willing to embrace the change that they speak about but also to be able to talk and, more importantly, lead from a place of experience.

3. **Show that you understand the value that already exists.** The word *change* terrifies some people because it makes them feel as if everything they are doing is totally irrelevant. Rarely is that the case. It is great to share new ideas, but when you honor the person and tap into what exists, this is more powerful. When you show people that you value them and their ideas in an authentic manner, they are more likely to move mountains and exceed expectations. A strengths-based approach should not only be reserved for our students. If we want others to move forward, identifying the value they already have is helpful to not only their growth but our own as well.

4. **Share your stories.** Evidence should inform what we do and is an important part of the change process, but the emotional connection we make to the significance is often what drives people toward purposeful change. The impact of our stories is crucial to helping move people forward.

Stories are the fuel for innovation, especially in a world where there is so much information. As author Daniel Pink shares,

Stories are easier to remember because stories are how we remember. When facts become so widely available and instantly accessible, each one becomes less valuable. What begins to matter more is the ability to place these facts in context and to deliver them with emotional impact.[1]

If the thoughts bring you to emotion, they are more likely to stick out in your memory, and you are more likely to act.

If you want to help people embrace a new narrative, the best way is to create that new narrative together. What is the story of your classroom, school, or organization? Not just the story of the past, but what is the story you will write together in the future? People are more likely to connect with a story if they can visualize themselves in it.

To influence others and bring about change, simply being knowledgeable is not enough. People who actually know less about the technical aspects of content or specific classroom practices can be more influential and move others to create more change because of *how* they connect with and share *other people's* value and expertise. Making meaningful change in education is far less about the "stuff" and much more about the people. Tap into that, and you are more likely to see the change that you are hoping to see.

But What About . . .?

Innovation in education should not be a luxury; it is now a necessity. The world is changing so rapidly, and the need is no longer for schools to simply "embrace change" but to create it. I hear from educators often about the many "obstacles" that stand in the way of them making the changes that they want to see. Their questions follow a pattern that sounds like this: "I think innovation is important but what about . . . (insert curriculum, time, money, standardized tests, and lack of training, etc.)?"

I'm not denying that challenges exist. Remember the title of this book? *Innovate Inside the Box*. I believe the challenges educators face are the main reason innovation is necessary. When we see so many constraints put upon the education system by sources outside of the educator's control, thinking outside of the box is not necessarily the best approach. How you innovate inside of the box is crucial.

As you hear each one of these arguments against innovation, it is important to have responses that help flip each on its head. Change the conversation and show how educators are already *being* innovative within the constraints.

1. What about the curriculum?

There are many textbooks and curricula around the world that are significantly outdated. To make matters worse, some of this outdated material actually includes more information and outcomes than the actual curriculum requires, so you are teaching more than you have to by following a textbook, which is a waste of time that could be better used to learn skills associated with outcomes. As a result, I have contended that curriculum should be co-constructed and flexible. You can still meet the standards (and likely more effectively) when you create learning experiences based on the context and needs of the learners, rather than on the static and dictated guidelines laid out by those removed from our classrooms.

At its best, the curriculum identifies resources and examples to support what you teach, not how. This is where "innovation" is brought to life. In one case, I read in the curriculum that students were to learn about the "fur trade" in Canada, and the suggested activity was to "listen to songs about the fur trade." *Hmmm.* There are many ways that you can still teach this objective, while bringing it to life. Why not a podcast, website, speech, or video? Creating opportunities for multiple means of engagement, representation, action and expression allows for more voice and choice, and empowers students to create, rather than simply consume, which is a huge step in the right direction.

How you look at the standards and curriculum is part of the idea of how innovation happens. Innovation is about teaching and learning in new and better ways in order to meet the needs of learners you serve. Innovation is not in your curriculum, but neither are worksheets. You choose how you bring your curriculum to life. That is the artistry of the work that we do.

> ## Innovation is not in your curriculum, but neither are worksheets. You choose how you bring your curriculum to life.

2. What about Standardized Tests?

Yup, you still have to do them. I could say, "Don't worry about them," but that is super easy for me to say as someone who doesn't teach in a traditional classroom anymore. I want you to understand this, however: Teaching to the test will not lead to the development of the knowledge, skills, and mindsets that are critical for success in a dynamic and changing world. Tests may be a reality in our system, but they are not your driver. Learners are.

If you take the advice on innovating *how* you teach your curriculum, the learning experience you create could actually help your students *do better* on whatever assessments they take. One high school teacher told me that the year she changed her teaching and became more innovative was the first year in her career that every student in her class passed the standardized test. The biggest change was the way she looked at her teaching and shifted the class into becoming more focused on *building relationships and creating empowering learning experiences.* Not only did her students do better on the tests, they actually had a better understanding of what they had learned and remembered it even after the test. They learned to learn, and that is the goal.

3. What about time?

Everyone reading this has the same amount of time in the day, and they also have things they do outside of school that they see as important. With the same amount of time, what differentiates one educator from another? Priority.

Make something a priority, and it will get done. (You get those report cards done every year, right?)

Working within the constraints of time requires that you think differently about what you do, and how you do it. For example, Katie Martin shared an example in her book, *Learner-Centered Innovation,* of how to restructure learning experiences to create more time for practice and feedback for students in class:

> *A teacher was spending thirty minutes daily teaching isolated grammar skills and an additional thirty minutes practicing spelling words. Instead, she reorganized the class time to allow students to write about their own ideas and incorporated spelling and grammar practice in authentic writing tasks together, and she created a thirty-minute block each day for students to get personal support and practice based on their needs. When the time in class was used for more*

personal support that allowed students time to prac-
tice and learn with peers and the teacher for support,
the need for homework was eliminated.

You will never be able to add more time to your day, nor should you try. Take this piece of advice I received early in my career: Shifting time to focus on how we can leverage our time for deeper and more authentic learning will always be beneficial to both students and teachers.

4. What about lack of training?

Here is the good news about learning in our world today. You can do as much of it as you want on any topic, and there is a ton of good stuff online for free. If you want to learn something badly enough, you can do that. I watched my niece learn to play complex songs on the drums within two weeks of getting a drum set for Christmas. She found her teachers on YouTube. If you want to learn, you can make it happen.

We will never be able to know it all, and we shouldn't be expected to. But we also can't let what we don't know hold us, or our students, back. There will never be enough time to learn all that we need to know, but how we think about how we use our time for professional learning can significantly change how our entire community grows in a year. If we are not seeking new and different learning experiences as educators, how can we expect anything different for our students? This is why it is crucial we create *new and better* solutions for how we create our own professional learning opportunities. How do you connect and collaborate with your peers? Do you invite others into your classroom to give you feedback, or do you visit other classrooms? How might you share what you are learning and make your learning process more visible? How can you innovate inside the box and ensure that it's not only about learning at certain points in the year or just fulfilling requirements, but having non-stop access to learn in times and ways that are meaningful to you, your peers, and the learners you serve?

Innovation is not a "thing" but a way of thinking. Like change, innovation isn't needed simply for the sake of innovation; it needs to happen because our world demands we create meaningful and deeper learning experiences in schools. It is not about just doing something new or using technology; it is about finding better ways to connect, teach, and learn. By altering the way we look at the challenges above (and many others that I haven't listed), we can shift from a mindset of obstacles to one of opportunities. This is the embodiment of the Innovator's Mindset.

Moving Forward

Change is hard. It's easy to get comfortable and just want to maintain the status quo. In parts of our lives, routine can be beneficial (going to bed at the same time, exercising daily, etc.). But as shared in *The Innovator's Mindset,* to innovate we must "disrupt our routine." This doesn't mean throwing out what already works but identifying what works and why, determining what we could improve, and trying new things that can make us even better. When it comes to the work we do in education and learning, change is part of the process. Change will forever be the only constant. We should not only learn how to survive change but to thrive through the process. That is what the learning process is about—continual growth and improvement.

As the referee taught me in those few moments on that basketball court all those years ago, we can choose to change our actions at any moment. As Maya Angelou says, "Do the best you can until you know better, and when you know better, do better." *You* have the ability to remake yourself or shift your thinking on any day. If you want to help others move forward, always remember that you have to go first. Lead from where you are, regardless of your title. That is how we are going to create an education system that meets the needs of the students we serve today.

Questions for Discussion

1. Identify one moment that you significantly changed your direction, personally or professionally. What happened and what change did you make because of it? Take the time to reflect and consider sharing it with colleagues.

2. What is the "story" of your classroom, school, or organization? What is the one you can tell, and what is the one you want to tell?

3. What are some of the "traditional" barriers to innovation in education, and how can you leverage them to create new and better opportunities for the learners you serve?

Please share to #InnovateInsideTheBox

Chapter 14
YOU ARE THE CORE

Our deepest fear is not that we are inadequate. Our deepest fear is that we are powerful beyond measure. It is our light, not our darkness, that most frightens us. We ask ourselves, "Who am I to be brilliant, gorgeous, talented, fabulous?" Actually, who are you not to be? You are a child of God. Your playing small does not serve the world. There is nothing enlightened about shrinking so that other people won't feel insecure around you. We are all meant to shine, as children do.

—Marianne Williamson

In this book, we have explored the Core of Innovative Teaching and Learning. We've considered strategies and looked at how connecting UDL and the Innovator's Mindset together can bring about amazing opportunities to innovate inside the box. These ideas are powerful, but none of them can ever be effective if you, yes *you*, are not in a space to be effective. *You* are the center of this work, whether you are a student, teacher, support staff, volunteer, or principal. You have the power to develop relationships that truly matter and can empower learners to become innovators, dreamers, and makers. If you work in schools and serve others, your well-being is crucial for this work. As the saying goes, you can't pour from an empty cup.

What do I mean by this? Here is an example from my experience:

As a principal, I remember a staff member who was struggling with some personal issues. Our work is deeply about being "human" and interpersonal connections, so when we struggle personally, it can have a negative impact on our effectiveness. I called her into my office to check on her, and she shared what was going on in her life. I will be honest; I don't think I could have dealt with her circumstances. Then I asked her, "Why are you here today?" She told me she was not sick, just struggling personally, so she thought she really couldn't take the day off. I told her that because she didn't have physical symptoms of an illness didn't mean she was in good health. Teachers are notoriously bad for not taking sick days. Some feel teacher-guilt, others believe it takes more effort to prepare for a substitute teacher than to just show up. I get it, and I have been there. I told her I would rather her be here this week for four days at 100 percent than five days at 50 percent. She understood and took some time, and when she came back, she looked like a new person.

If you work with an administrator who doesn't see mental health struggles the same as physical struggles, perhaps you are in a place that is not good for you. This one conversation with this teacher was not the exception. It was normal amongst the people I served, whether it was parents in the community, students dealing with personal things, or staff. As principal, I knew how important it was to be a shoulder to lean on for my community because my teachers were being that shoulder for so many of their students and their families.

Then one day, as I worked in central office, I had become emotionally fatigued and had a nervous breakdown. I was taking on the burden of others so much that I had forgotten to take care of myself, and I broke down. I reached out to my assistant superintendent, Kelly Wilkins, the best leader I have ever worked for, and I told her that I was struggling. She told me to go home and take as much time as I needed to get better. This was not a punishment but a reminder that when our job is about serving other people, we often forget to serve ourselves. I was nervous that taking time off to fix something that people couldn't "see" was a sign of weakness. Kelly reminded me, however, not asking for help was a sign of weakness. The fact that I was willing to ask for help was a sign of my strength.

> **When our job is about serving other people, we have to not forget to serve ourselves.**

I was embarrassed at first, and then realized that I *needed* some time. I knew that if I didn't do something about my mental health now, I might eventually quit the profession forever. When I came back to work, Kelly checked in on me and made me feel supported while also acting like nothing ever happened. She listened when I needed to be heard, and she talked when I asked for advice. If every educator had access to a leader like Kelly, the profession would be immeasurably better. As I was recovering, Kelly called me into her office and said, "Hey, we are talking over who we should bring in to keynote our entire division's opening day, and we thought, 'George does this in places all over the world; why not have someone from our own district?'" I was blown away by the offer, and, to be honest, surprised. I literally was crying in Kelly's office only a few weeks earlier, and then she brings me in to entrust me with a massive opportunity to speak in front of my whole staff. I was nervous to accept, but Kelly knew I was ready for the task. She saw and utilized my strengths and put me in a position that empowered and encouraged me. Opening day came and, I will tell you, up until that point, that was the best keynote I had ever done. I had put so much into it because of Kelly's belief in me. When we see and treat each other as humans first, and educators second, everyone benefits.

So what does this story have to do with innovation in education? Everything.

We aren't likely to be innovative in jobs we hate or in which we don't feel valued. We also cannot work with excellence if we don't take care of ourselves physically and mentally. Compassion fatigue is legitimate, and, yes, you might be able to get far with it, but it will catch up. Understand that you and the relationships you create are the core of teaching and learning. Government initiatives, district initiatives, wherever initiatives, they will come and go, but people like you and me and our colleagues and students comprise the system.

I wish that I thought more about my own personal well-being earlier in my career. Here are some things I wish I knew then that I hope will help strengthen you today to help others:

1. **Understand that some days will not work out the way you want them to, so it is okay to start again tomorrow.** I have had bad days as a teacher and administrator and as a human. You can go home and cry (you will sometimes) and be frustrated, but there is always the next day. You will not have to get the most out of every kid, every single day. Think of it this way: If one of your students has a bad day, would you push them to stay at school until the day turned "good"? Or would you perhaps encourage them to step back and start again tomorrow? The ability to "get back up" is something we want to teach our kids, so it is okay to do the same. Sometimes walking away, taking a break, doing something else, and starting again tomorrow is the best thing to do.

2. **Your students look up to you, but that doesn't mean you need to be perfect.** In their post, "Dear New Teachers, You Don't Need to Be Superheroes," Trevor Muir and John Spencer share the following advice: "You don't have to be perfect. Teaching is a craft that takes years to master, and even then, you'll continue to make mistakes. And that's okay."[1]

   Being vulnerable and showing that you are a person not only makes you more relatable but more realistic to your students. If you are having a bad day, that is okay. I remember sharing with my students how hard it was when I lost my first dog. I was okay crying in front of them and was quite upset, and they rallied around me and checked in on me for weeks after. I promise you; we only had a better connection after this moment because they knew that even adults have tough times. My kids showed tremendous empathy for what I was going through. In a world that is becoming more digital, being human is more important than ever.

> In a world that is becoming more digital, being human is more important than ever.

3. **"What are you doing for students that they can be doing themselves?"** I know I shared the above quote from A.J. Juliani and John Spencer earlier in the book, but it is worth sharing again. Here is the deal in teaching and leading: The more you micromanage people, the more work it is for you. I know many educators who spend way too many late nights at schools trying to plan the "perfect" lesson for students, but there

is no such thing. Teaching is exceptionally hard work, and sometimes we make it harder by over-planning our teaching and under-planning their learning. Find ways to give more ownership to students in their learning and the classroom or school.

4. **Never assume someone is "good." Reach out and check in on people, no matter their demeanor**. Some of the people that seem the happiest or "most successful" are struggling in ways we can't see. We sometimes put on a brave face when times are toughest, and sharing a kind word or acknowledgment has zero risk, where not sharing one is a missed opportunity. Sharing gratitude of others is a way to fill your own bucket, as selfish as that may seem.

5. **Breaks are good for you. Take them and enjoy them**. I don't listen to education podcasts. I listen to sports podcasts. I have limited my use of social media on the weekend for education purposes. Do you know why? Because I need a break. So do you. And there is evidence that breaks will make you better at what you do, long term.[2] Teacher-guilt is a real thing and not beneficial. Growth is essential to all educators, but the focus on growth all of the time can and will lead to burnout.

Here's another little tip on taking breaks: If someone outside of education makes a condescending comment about how teachers get "two months off for summer," maybe respond with, "We do, and it is glorious!" My gut is that they don't see all the work that educators do during breaks, evenings, weekends, and no matter what you tell them, some aren't willing to listen. So rub it in their face a bit. We know that narrative is false, but making that comment might feel good for a few minutes. :) I have learned that if sometimes you don't laugh, you will cry. Sometimes a sense of humor is the best way to deal with a lack of knowledge about what teachers *truly* do, not only for our students but for society as a whole.

But just as a reminder . . . there is only one you, and we need you to take care of yourself.

What Is Your Compelling Reason?

While we do need to take care of ourselves, we need to remember why we got into the profession in the first place. Teachers go into education because they know they can have an impact on children's lives—an impact that no administrator or government agency will ever be able to fully measure. The minutiae of the day-to-day working within education—things no one ever warned us about in teacher college—can make us forget that purpose and lose our passion. That's what had happened to me. Thankfully, I was blessed to have moved to a new school where Kelly Wilkins saved my career and changed my life.

I've since learned that to thrive in education we have to find inspiration in ourselves. People like Kelly won't always be there to save the day. But we can always step back, shift our thinking, and find our way back to our why. It is not always easy, but it is always possible.

When I get to speak to educators, I often share a video that depicts an older man who is learning to read for the first time. The story touches my heart every time. In it, the older gentleman does things that many of our elementary students do to improve their reading and grow as learners. He connects with his friends and partner, and his excitement grows as he sees his own development. Later in the video, he opens a large book and starts reading it voraciously. He reads it every chance he can get, and eventually finishes it. He then walks into a pub, walks up to a young man who addresses him as "Dad" and says, "Hey, Tubbs, I read your book." The son, in a voice of surprise replies, "You read my book?" The father nods to the son, the son tears up, and then they share a warm embrace. It is a beautiful moment.

Whenever I share this video, tears flow freely from the audience and from myself. I'm not talking about tears welling up in our eyes; I'm talking about ugly crying. That's when I turn down the sound on the video and point out that all the people crying in the audience are actually crying to a Scotch commercial (Bell's Whisky South Africa). Sure enough, we watch as father and son raise a glass to one another. I don't drink often, but something about that video makes me want to have a scotch. The ugly crying then turns to laughter. *All that crying for a scotch commercial?!* It is a beautiful thing to see and reminds me of my hope for each interaction with educators as summarized by the late basketball coach, Jim Valvano, to make people "laugh, think, and cry." This single video does all of those things.

I show that video for two reasons. The first is to point out that the growth we saw in this gentleman was powerful enough to make us all cry over a scotch commercial. How would people feel if they saw the beautiful stories educators all over the world are witness to every single day, the ones that we take for granted because we see them all of the time in our schools? Who better to change the narrative of education than educators themselves? That's the first lesson: Our stories are essential.

But there is another, more personal, reason I share this video. The gentleman learning to read reminds me a lot of my own mom. An immigrant to Canada with very limited formal education, she had a tutor come and teach her to read English. She was in her fifties and sixties at the time. Why, at such a late age, would my mom want to take up reading? Because she knew her kids wrote, and she wanted to be able to read what they shared with others. I guarantee you my mom has read my first book more than any other human being, not because she is passionate about the content but because she is passionate about her son. My parents, through their actions, taught me this over and over again: When you have a compelling reason, you can learn anything.

I hope Katie and I have provided you not only with strategies to serve your students but, more importantly, with a compelling reason to continue to grow for those you serve. Let's make sure we help the students we serve find their compelling reason as well.

> **When you have a compelling reason, you can learn anything.**

Thank you for all that you do to inspire students around the world, but in that process, just a reminder: don't forget to inspire yourself. We need you.

Questions for Discussion

Think back to the original three questions from the introduction:

1. What has challenged you?
2. What has been reaffirmed?
3. What will you do moving forward?

Take some time to reflect, either privately or publicly, on these questions. The most important question of these three is the last. We would love to hear what you will do to move to action.

Please share to #InnovateInsideTheBox

BIBLIOGRAPHY

Because of a Teacher

1. Street, Elizabeth. "The Moving Story of How a Teacher Inspired Maya Angelou to Speak." Estreet. *K12 Learning Lift Off*. May 8, 2017. learningliftoff.com/ how-a-teacher-inspired-maya-angelou-to-speak.

2. Gates, Bill. "A Teacher Who Changed My Life." *Gates Notes*. August 16, 2016. gatesnotes.com/ Education/A-Teacher-Who-Changed-My-Life.

3. Carter, Maria. "Elementary School Janitor Leaves Cute Messages in the Carpet Overnight." *Woman's Day*. November 11, 2016. womansday.com/life/a56945/ janitor-leaves-cute-messages-in-carpet-overnight.

4. Brock, Annie and Heather Hundley, *The Growth Mindset Coach: A Teacher's Month-by-Month Handbook for Empowering Students to Achieve*. Berkeley, California: Ulysses Press, 2016.

Chapter 1

1. Klein, Allison. "This elementary school principal reads books on Facebook to ensure her students have a bedtime story." *The Washington Post Online*. March 1, 2019. washingtonpost.com/lifestyle/2019/03/01/why-this-principal-gets-into-pjs-reads-bedtime-stories-facebook-live-her-students-night/?utm_term=.5ba797312d27.

2. Cook, C. R., Fiat, A., Larson, M., Daikos, C., Slemrod, T., Holland, E. A., . . . Renshaw, T. "Positive Greetings at the Door: Evaluation of a Low-Cost, High-Yield Proactive Classroom Management Strategy." *Journal of Positive Behavior Interventions, 20*(3), (2018): 149–159.

3. Baker, J. Grant, s., and Morlock, L. "The teacher–student relationship as a developmental context for children with internalizing or externalizing behavior problems." *School Psychology Quarterly, 23*(1). (2008): 3-15.

4. O'Connor, E. E., Dearing, E., and Collins, B. A. "Teacher-child relationship and behavior problem trajectories in elementary school." *American Educational Research Journal*, 48(1), (2011): 120-162.

5. Silver, R. B., Measelle, J. R., Armstrong, J. M., and Essex, M. J. "Trajectories of classroom externalizing behavior: Contributions of child characteristics, family characteristics, and the teacher–child relationship during the school transition." *Journal of School Psychology*, 43(1), (2005): 39-60.

6. Midgley, C., Feldlaufer, H., and Eccles, J. S. "Student/teacher relations and attitudes toward mathematics before and after the transition to junior high school." *Child Development*, (1989): 981-992.

7. The Ohio State University. "Why Relationships–Not Money–Are the Key to improving schools: Study finds social capital has 3-5 times the impact of funding." *Science Daily*. October 25, 2018. sciencedaily.com/releases/2018/10/181025103300.htm.

8. Gustafson, Brad. *Reclaiming Our Calling: Hold on to the Heart, Mind, and Hope of Education*. San Diego, California: Impress: 2018.

9. Pierson, Rita. "Every Kid Needs a Champion." *TED Talks Education*. May 2013. ted.com/talks/rita_pierson_every_kid_needs_a_champion.

Chapter 2

1. Matyszczyk, Chris. "Google: GPAs Are Worthless," *Cnet*. June 20, 2013. cnet.com/news/google-gpas-are-worthless.

2. Baker, Suzanne. "Student petition says too much pressure to succeed at Naperville North," *Chicago Tribune*. April 14, 2017.

3. Sinek, Simon. *Start with Why: How Great Leaders Inspire Everyone to Take Action*. New York: Portfolio, 2009.

4. Shareski, Dean. "Stop Following Your Passions . . . the Celebration of Work." *Ideas and Thoughts*. ideasandthoughts.org/2012/08/22/ stop-following-your-passions-the-celebration-of-work.

5. Martin, Katie. "What Questions Are Learners Asking?" *KatieLMartin.com*, September 13, 2017. katielmartin. com/2017/09/13/what-questions-are-learners-asking.

6. Haller, Sonja. "YouTube's Top Earner is a 7-year-old who made $22 million playing with toys." *USA Today*. December 5, 2018. usatoday.com/story/life/allthemoms/2018/12/05/ youtube-top-earner-7-year-old-made-22-million-playing-toys/2206508002.

7. Iaones, Ellen. "7-year-old YouTuber to get his own show on Nickelodeon." *The Daily Dot*. February 16, 2019. dailydot. com/upstream/ryan-toysreview-youtube.

8. Louden, Kristy. "Delaying the Grade: How to Get Students to Read Feedback." *Cult of Pedagogy*. June 4, 2017. cultofpedagogy.com/delayed-grade.

9. Miller, Brandon. "Can Focusing on Strengths Really Make a Difference?" *34 Strong*. March 16, 2015. 34strong.com/the-clifton-strengthsfinder-can-focusing-on-strengths-really-make-a-difference.

10. Den Heijer, Alexander. "Quotes by Alxander Den Heijer." *alexanderdenheijer.com* alexanderdenheijer.com/quotes.

11. Richardson, Will. "Curiosity Is the Cat." *WillRichardson.com*. February 11, 2017. willrichardson.com/curiosity-is-the-cat.

12. McQuaid, Michelle. "Ten Reasons to Focus on Your Strengths." *Psychology Today*. November11, 2014. psychologytoday.com/ ca/blog/functioning-flourishing/201411/ ten-reasons-focus-your-strengths.

Chapter 3

1. Knodel, Lisa. "Forbes 30 Under 30 Includes Mason Student: Her Device Generates Green Energy." *Journal News*. January 31, 2017. journal-news.com/news/local/forbes-under-includes-mason-student/F0Hi79qHyZ7IquVSgBSaHO.

2. Friedman, Thomas L. *Thank You for Being Late: An Optimist's Guide for Thriving in the Age of Accelerations*. New York: Picador, 2017.

3. Spencer, John and A.J. Juliani. *Empower: What Happens When Students Own Their Learning*. San Diego, California: IMPress, 2017.

4. Parrot, Kiera. "Thinking Outside the Bin: Why Labeling Books by Reading Level Disempowers Young Readers." *School Library Journal*. August 28, 2017. slj.com/?detailStory=thinking-outside-the-bin-why-labeling-books-by-reading-level-disempowers-young-readers.

5. Berger, Warren and Michael Quinlan. *A More Beautiful Question: The Power of Inquiry to Spark Breakthrough Ideas*. New York: Bloomsbury, 2014.

6. Lang, Amanda. *The Power of Why*. New York: New York: Collins, 2017.

7. Couros, George. "Taking Notes vs. Taking a Picture of Notes. Which Wins?" *The Principal of Change*. August 23, 1015: georgecouros.ca/blog/archives/5505.

8. Zhao, Yong. Conference Keynote. TIES, Minneapolis, Minnesota, 2014.

9. Martin, Katie. *Learner-Centered Innovation: Spark Curiosity, Ignite Passion, and Unleash Genius*. San Diego, California: IMPress, 2018.

10. Couros, George. *The Innovator's Mindset: Empower Learning, Unleash Talent, and Lead a Culture of Creativity*. San Diego, California: Dave Burgess Consulting, 2015.

11. Spencer, John and A.J. Juliani. *Empower: What Happens When Students Own Their Learning.* San Diego, California: IMPress, 2017.

Chapter 4

1. Hess, Frederick M. "No, educators and policy makers should not just 'do what the research shows.'" *Medium: Education.* June 5, 2018. medium.com/@rickhess99/no-educators-and-policymakers-shouldnt-just-do-what-the-research-shows-6c0e9664893a.

2. Richardson, Will. "On Learning . . . in School." *Willrichardson.com.* March 12, 2019. *willrichardson*.com/on-learning-in-school.

3. TeachThought Staff. "The First Six Weeks: Strategies for Getting to Know Your Students." *TeachThought.* October 9, 2018. teachthought.com/pedagogy/the-first-6-weeks-strategies-for-getting-to-know-your-students.

4. Smith, Rick or Mary Lambert. "Assuming the Best." *Educational Leadership, ASCD.* ascd.org/publications/educational-leadership/sept08/vol66/num01/Assuming-the-Best.aspx.

5. Mikkelsen, Kenneth and Harold Jarche. "The Best Leaders Are Constant Learners." Harvard Business Review. October 16, 2015. hbr.org/2015/10/the-best-leaders-are-constant-learners.

6. Simmons, Michael. "Bill Gates, Warren Buffet, and Oprah All Use the 5-Hour Rule." *Medium: Accelerated Intelligence.* July 22, 2016. medium.com/accelerated-intelligence/bill-gates-warren-buffett-and-oprah-all-use-the-5-hour-rule-308f528b6363.

Part Two Introduction

1. Meyer, Ann, David H. Rose, and David Gordon. *Universal Design for Learning: Theory and Practice.* udltheorypractice.cast.org.

Chapter 5

1. "Empathy." *Lexico.com.* lexico.com/en/definition/empathy

2. sitwithus.io/#!/About.

3. "About Sit With Us." youtube.com/watch?v=sh7XFCysTr4

4. Miller, Jeff."Master This 1 Quality to Make Your Team Happier and More Productive." *Inc.com.* January 9, 2019. inc.com/jeff-miller/studies-show-empathy-is-an-essential-quality-for-leaders-heres-how-to-master-it.html

5. Catapano, Jordan. "Teaching Strategies: The Importance of Empathy." *TeachHub.com.* teachhub.com/teaching-strategies-importance-empathy

6. "For Educators: How to Build Empathy and Strengthen Your School Community." *Harvard Graduate School of Education.* mcc.gse.harvard.edu/resources-for-educators/how-build-empathy-strengthen-school-community.

7. Borba, M. Nine Competencies for Teaching Empathy: An educational psychologist and parenting expert offers advice to school leaders. *Educational Leadership*, 76(2), (2018): 22.

8. Brown, Brené. "List of Core Emotions." brenebrown.com/wp-content/uploads/2018/03/List-of-Core-Emotions-2018.pdf

9. "Summer Language Exploration." *Groton-Dunstable High School.* gdrsd.org/gdrhs/students/summer-language-exploration.

Chapter 6

1. McIntosh, Ewan. "TEDx London: The Problem Finders." Video: 8:00. November 29, 2011. edu.blogs.com/edublogs/2011/11/tedxlondon-the-problem-finders-video.html.

2. Weller, Chris. "The 10 Most Important Inventors Under 18." *Business Insider.* May 20, 2016. businessinsider.com/the-greatest-inventors-under-18-2016-5/

3. safewander.com.

4. Kenneth Shinozuka–Created socks for Alzheimer's patients that alert family members when a relative strays from bed." *Business Insider*. businessinsider.com/the-greatest-inventors-under-18-2016-5#kenneth-shinozuka–created-socks-for-alzheimers-patients-that-alert-family-members-when-a-relative-strays-from-bed-4.

5. Maiers, Angela. "Forget Following Your Heart–Follow Your Heartbreak." *AngelaMaiers.com*. angelamaiers.com/blog/forget-following-your-heart-follow-your-heartbreak.html.

6. Yazzie-Mintz, E. *Charting the Path from Engagement to Achievement: A Report on the 2009 High School Survey of Student Engagement*. Bloomington, Indiana: Center for evaluation and education policy, 2010.

7. *Pages for Peace Project*. pagesforpeace.org/home.

8. Novak, Katie and Kristan Rodriguez. "UDL Progression Rubric." Wakefield, Massachusetts: CAST, 2018. castpublishing.org/wp-content/uploads/2018/02/UDL_Progression_Rubric_FINAL_Web_REV1.pdf

Chapter 7

1. Grant, Adam and Sheryl Sandberg. *Originals: How Non-Conformists Move the World*. New York: Penguin, 2016.

2. Meyer, Ann, David H. Rose, and David Gordon. *Universal Design for Learning: Theory and Practice*. udltheorypractice.cast.org

3. "DESE Model Feedback Instruments & Administration Protocols." *MDESE*. doe.mass.edu/edeval/feedback/surveys.html.

4. Herrera, Tim. "Do you keep a Failure Résumé? Here's Why You Should Start." *The New York Times*. February 3, 2019. nytimes.com/2019/02/03/smarter-living/failure-resume.html.

Chapter 8

1. Lowry, Mary Pauline. "This Is How One Sixth Grade Girl Helped Improve Flint's Water Crisis." *The Oprah Magazine.* December 11, 2018. oprahmag.com/life/a25383285/mari-copeny-barack-obama-flint-water-crisis.

2. "10,000+ Backpacks Filled with School Supplies to Be Distributed in Flint, MI." *Cision PR Newswire.* July 25, 2018. prnewswire.com/news-releases/10-000-backpacks-filled-with-school-supplies-to-be-distributed-in-flint-mi-300686518.html.

3. McCarthy, Joe. "This 10-Year-Old Just Delivered 135,000 Bottles of Water to Flint Residents." *Global Citizen.* June 5, 2018. globalcitizen.org/en/content/10-year-old-little-miss-flint-water-mari-copeny.

4. Gallucci, Nicole. "Little Miss Flint's 5 Awesome Tips for Becoming a Young Activist." *Mashable.* September 22, 2018. mashable.com/article/little-miss-flint-mari-copeny-how-to-be-a-young-activist/#GE0OrtOhUgq5.

5. Couros, George. Digital Leadership Defined." *The Principal of Change.* January 7, 2013. georgecouros.ca/blog/archives/3584.

6. Greenfield, Rebecca. "Brainstorming Doesn't Work; Try This Technique Instead." *Fast Company.* July, 29, 2014. fastcompany.com/3033567/brainstorming-doesnt-work-try-this-technique-instead.

7. Cain, Susan. *Quiet: The Power of Introverts in a World That Can't Stop Talking.* Broadway Books, 2013.

8. "ECET2 Participants Give Advice to New Participants." *Bill & Melinda Gates Foundation.* k12education.gatesfoundation.org/blog/ecet2.

9. Transforming urban education: Collaborating to produce success in science, mathematics and technology education, Chapter: 11, Publisher: Sense Netherlands, Editors: Kenneth Tobin, Ashraf Shady, pp.181-190.

10. Anderson, Peter. "So, What'd You Think? Asking Students about My Lessons." *Mr. Anderson Reads & Writes*. January 19, 2017. mrandersonwrites.wordpress.com/2017/01/19/so-whatd-you-like-asking-students-about-my-lessons.

11. "Making Learning Personalized & Customized." Video, *Tch Teaching Channel*: 12:16. teachingchannel.org/video/workshop-model-customized-learning.

Chapter 9

1. "The NCTE Definition of 21st Century Literacies." *National Council of Teachers of English*. February 28, 2013. www2.ncte.org/statement/21stcentdefinition.

2. Widrich, Leo. "Why We Have Our Best Ideas in the Shower: The Science of Creativity." *Buffer*. open.buffer.com/shower-thoughts-science-of-creativity.

3. Kaplan, Elle. "Why Negative People Are Literally Killing You (and How to Protect Your Positivity)." *The Mission*. 15 Nov. 2016, medium.com/the-mission/why-negative-people-are-literally-killing-you-and-how-to-obliterate-pessimism-from-your-life-eb85fadced87.

4. Ulmer , Mikaila, "Our Sweet Story." *Me and the Bees*. meandthebees.com/pages/about-us.

5. Jeffrey, James. "The 13-Year-Old Who Built a Best-Selling Lemonade Brand." *BBC News*. July 23, 2018. bbc.com/news/business-44860428.

6. Oguz-Unver, A., and Yurumezoglu, K. A Teaching Strategy for Developing the Power of Observation in Science Education. Online Submission, (2009): 105–119.

7. Canpolat, M., Kuzu, S., Yildirim, B., and Canpolat, S. Active Listening Strategies of Academically Successful University Students. *Eurasian Journal of Educational Research*, (60), (2015): 163–180.

Chapter 10

1. "RyanMcHenry." *Wikipedia*. en.wikipedia.org/wiki/Ryan_McHenry.

2. @RyanGosling, *Twitter*. May 4, 2015.

3. @RyanGosling, *Twitter*. May 4, 2015.

4. Friedman, Thomas L. "How to Get a Job at Google." *The New York Times*. February 22, 2014. nytimes. com/2014/02/23/opinion/sunday/friedman-how-to-get-a-job-at-google.html.

5. "Internet Culture." *Wikipedia*.

6. Schleicher, Joel. Keynote Speech, ISTE 2018.

7. Spencer, John. "The Surprising Truth Behind Creating and Consuming." *Different by Design*. February 25, 2019. spencerauthor.com/critical-consuming.

8. Gonzalez, Jennifer. "Is That Higher-Order Task Really Higher-Order?" *Cult of Pedagogy*. May 12, 2019. cultofpedagogy.com/higher-order.

9. Brown, Brene. *Daring Greatly: How the Courage to Be Vulnerable Transforms the Way We Live, Love, Parent, and Lead*. Avery, 2012.

10. Schwartz, Barry. "The Paradox of Choice." TEDGlobal 2005. Video, 19:33. ted.com/talks/barry_schwartz_on_the_paradox_of_choice/transcript.

11. Iyengar, Sheena. "How Much Choice Is Too Much? Determinants of Individual Contributions in 401K Retirement Plans." *Pension Design and Structure: New Lessons from Behavioral Finance*. Ed. O. S. Mitchell and S. P. Utkus. New York: Oxford University Press, 2004.

12. Marquis, E., and Vajoczki, S. Creative Differences: Teaching Creativity across the Disciplines. *International Journal for the Scholarship of Teaching and Learning*, 6(1). (2012).

Chapter 11

1. Kennedy, John R. "John Carrey Reflects on Father in Iowa Commencement Speech." *Global News*. May 26, 2014. globalnews.ca/news/1353984/jim-carrey-reflects-on-father-in-iowa-commencement-speech.

2. Volpitta, Donna. "The Importance of Resilience for Kids With Learning and Attention Issues." understood.org/en/friends-feelings/empowering-your-child/building-on-strengths/the-importance-of-resilience-for-kids-with-learning-and-attention-issues.

3. Juliani, A.J. The Big Difference Between Failing and Fail-ure." *A.J. Juliani.* ajjuliani.com/big-difference-fail-ing-fail-ure.

4. Sandberg, Sheryl and Adam Grant. *Option B: Facing Adversity, Building Resilience, and Finding Joy.* New York: Knopf, 2017.

5. Gould-Born, James. "High School Student Secretly Draws All 411 of His Graduating Classmates." *Bored Panda.* boredpanda.com/high-school-student-secretly-draws-graduation-portraits-boston-latin-school-phillip-sossou/?utm_source=google&utm_medium=organic&utm_campaign=organic.

6. "Spanx Founder Sarah Blakely's Favorite Mistake." *Newsweek.* June 25, 2019. newsweek.com/spanx-founder-sara-blakelys-favorite-mistake-64113.

Chapter 12

1. Immordino-Yang, Mary Helen. "Rest Is Not Idleness: Reflection Is Critical for Development and Well-Being." *Association for Psychological Science.* psychologicalscience.org/news/releases/rest-is-not-idleness-reflection-is-critical-for-development-and-well-being.html.

2. Willimon, Will. "The Importance of Daydreaming." *Time.* May 23, 2014. time.com/110304/the-importance-of-daydreaming.

3. Stevens, Sidney. "5 Ways Daydreaming Is Good for You." *Mother Nature Network.* October 26, 2017. mnn.com/health/fitness-well-being/stories/5-ways-daydreaming-is-good-for-you.

4. Costa, Arthur L. and Bena Kallick. *Learning and Leading with Habits of Mind.* ASCD, 2008. ascd.org/publications/books/108008/chapters/Learning-Through-Reflection.aspx.

5. Kail, Col. Eric. "Leadership Character: The Role of Reflection." *The Washington Post.* March 9, 2012. washingtonpost.com/blogs/guest-insights/post/leadership-character-the-role-of-reflection/2011/04/04/gIQAdJOr1R_blog.html?utm_term=.cacd8a1ed00f.

6. Anderson, Mike. *Learning to Choose, Choosing to Learn: The Key to Student Motivation and Achievement.* ASCD, 2016.

7. "Highlighting Mistakes: A Grading Strategy." *The Teaching Channel.* Video: 07:26. teachingchannel.org/video/math-test-grading-tips.

Chapter 13

1. Stevenson, Doug. "Storytelling and Brain Science: This Is Your Brain on Story." *Association for Talent Development.* July 26, 2016. td.org/insights/storytelling-and-brain-science-this-is-your-brain-on-story.

Chapter 14

1. Spencer, John. "Dear New Teachers, You Don't Need to Be Superheroes." SpencerAuthor.com. March 6, 2019. spencerauthor.com/teacher-superheroes.

2. Selig, Meg. "How Do Work Breaks You're your Brain? 5 Surprising Answers." *Psychology Today.* April 18, 2017. psychologytoday.com/us/blog/changepower/201704/how-do-work-breaks-help-your-brain-5-surprising-answers.

ACKNOWLEDGMENTS

From George Couros

I had no intention of writing a second book and then I met Katie Novak. We immediately connected in a fifteen minute face-to-face conversation, and she somehow gave me the courage to write again. She inspires me with her intelligence, work-ethic (she works some weird hours), and how she does it all with endless kindness and humor. I have learned so much from you in this process and it was truly a blessing to my life the day we met and now you are stuck with me.

To Katie Martin, one of my dearest friends in the world and she always finds the perfect balance of challenging me to grow while finding a way to make clearer what I am trying to say. This book would not have happened without her guidance and support.

To Dave and Shelley Burgess. Thank you for believing in me and so many others while amplifying their voice in education. Your impact on education is immeasurable and I am beyond grateful for your guidance and friendship.

To Meghan Lawson (Megatron), thank you for your help with this book. You see things I don't, and I appreciate you always having a laser-like focus on serving kids and adults to make education better for every person that enters a school.

To the IMPress team, thank you for all that you did to put this book together. You reminded me that no one does anything on their own.

To all the educators in the world, thank you for all that you do that has inspired this book to come together. Your stories inspire me daily.

To my brothers and sister, thank you for always looking out for your baby brother.

To my dad, I miss you. Thank you for all that you did to provide every opportunity for your kids to find their own way.

To my mom, thank you for believing in me. You have been there for me more than anyone in the world. I am proud to say that I am a mama's boy.

To my wife Paige, thank you for all of your support when you know I often struggle. You are a rock and the best mom and teacher I have ever met.

And to my daughter Kallea. You are my heart.

From Katie Novak

Sometimes in life, you meet people and you know instantly that you were meant to be a part of each other's world. George and I gave back-to-back keynotes at a statewide conference in California. During the transition, we passed each other and started chatting. The rest, they say, is history. Since that moment, we have continued to build on each other's crazy ideas and have created something pretty special. George, thanks for being one of my professional soulmates.

To Lindie, my fabulous sister and business partner, you are my best friend, my muse, my travel companion, and the best darn mixologist I've ever met. Thank you for organizing me, inspiring me, and making me laugh more than anyone. Also, thanks for being an incredible partner in the game, Taboo. We could easily win the world championship. Love you, sister.

Of course, thank you to Paige Couros, Katie Martin, and the IMPress team, even though George stole my thunder on that one.

To mom and dad. Congrats on forty-five years together. You make love look easy and you make parenting look even easier. Thank you for everything, even the month long cross country trip where Dad threatened to leave me in Yellowstone. xoxox

To Lon, the love of my life. Thank you for bringing me dog toys, instead of flowers, on our first date. Thank you for letting me be me - always. You are my biggest fan, my greatest supporter, and the best steel drum player and Olympic luger I have ever seen. Our four collaborative projects (that's a great euphemism!), Torin, Aylin, Brecan, and Boden, are my proudest creations. Every single day, I recognize how blessed I am to have created this incredible life with you.

TO FURTHER YOUR LEARNING

If you want to dive into these topics more, check out these books from the authors and IMPress:

The Innovator's Mindset

Empower Learning, Unleash Talent, and Lead a Culture of Creativity

By George Couros

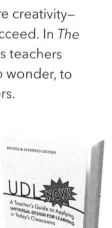

The traditional system of education requires students to hold their questions and compliantly stick to the scheduled curriculum. But our job as educators is to provide new and better opportunities for our students. It's time to recognize that compliance doesn't foster innovation, encourage critical thinking, or inspire creativity—and those are the skills our students need to succeed. In *The Innovator's Mindset*, George Couros encourages teachers and administrators to empower their learners to wonder, to explore—and to become forward-thinking leaders.

UDL Now!

A Teacher's Guide to Applying UNIVERSAL DESIGN FOR LEARNING in Today's Classroom

By Katie Novak

In *UDL Now!*, Katie Novak provides practical insights and savvy strategies for helping all learners excel in inclusive classrooms. She shares how to use Universal Design for Learning (UDL) to plan meaningful, authentic learning experiences where all students are partners in the design and delivery of their education. *UDL Now!* is a fun and effective Monday-morning playbook for powerful teaching.

Empower

*What Happens When Students Own
Their Learning*

By A.J. Juliani and John Spencer

In an ever-changing world, educators and
parents must take a role in helping students
prepare themselves for *anything.* That
means unleashing their creative potential! In
Empower, A.J. Juliani and John Spencer provide teachers,
coaches, and administrators with a roadmap that will inspire
innovation, authentic learning experiences, and practical
ways to empower students to pursue their passions while
in school.

Learner-Centered Innovation

*Spark Curiosity, Ignite Passion, and
Unleash Genius*

By Katie Martin

Learning opportunities and teaching methods
must evolve to match the ever-changing
needs of today's learners. In *Learner-Centered
Innovation,* Katie Martin offers insights into
how to make the necessary shifts and create an environment
where learners at every level are empowered to take risks in
pursuit of learning and growth rather than perfection.

Take the L.E.A.P.

Ignite a Culture of Innovation

By Elizabeth Bostwick

Take the L.E.A.P.: Ignite a Culture of Innovation will inspire and support you as you to take steps to grow beyond traditional and self-imposed boundaries. Award-winning educator Elisabeth Bostwick shares stories and practical strategies to help you challenge conventional thinking and create the conditions that empower meaningful learning.

Drawn to Teach

An Illustrated Guide to Transforming Your Teaching

Written by Josh Stumpenhorst, Illustrated by Trevor Guthke

If you're looking for ways to help your students succeed, you won't find the answer in gimmicks, trends, or fads. Great teaching isn't about test results or data; it's about connecting with students and empowering them to own their learning. Through this clever, illustrated guide, Josh Stumpenhorst reveals the key characteristics all top educators share in common and shows you how to implement them in your teaching practice.

ABOUT THE AUTHORS

George Couros has been involved with education for over 20 years and has focused on the areas of innovative leadership, teaching, and learning. He has worked at all levels of K-12 education as a teacher, technology facilitator, and school and district administrator. He is a sought after speaker on the topic of innovative leadership, student learning and empowerment and has worked with schools and organizations around the world and is the author of the best-selling book, "The Innovator's Mindset." Although George is a leader in the area of innovation, his focus is always on the development of leadership and people and what is best for learners. His belief is that if you want to inspire meaningful change, you will have to make a connection to the heart before you make a connection to the mind and he lives by the Jim Valvano credo that you need to "cry, laugh, and think" every single day, and often does some of those things more than others. He is also a husband and proud father to his daughter Kallea and two dogs (Odom and Cooper).

You can connect with George on his blog, "The Principal of Change" (located at georgecouros.ca) or through Twitter and Instagram (@gcouros).

Katie Novak, EdD is an inter-nationally renowned education consultant as well as a practicing leader in education as an Assistant Superintendent of Schools in Massachusetts. With 16 years of experience in teaching and admin-istration, an earned doctorate in curriculum and teaching, and five books published (this is lucky #6), including the best-selling UDL

Now!, Katie designs and presents workshops both nationally and internationally focusing on implementation of Universal Design for Learning (UDL), building effective systems that work for all learners, and universally designed leadership.

Novak's grandmother once told her, "Never stop fighting for something." Believing in, honoring, and advocating for every sin-gle learner has become hers. As a proud Momma of 4 humans and one grumpy old dog, Emerson, she hopes to create warriors who recognize the brilliance of every individual they meet. When she's not involved in all things edu, she loves woodworking, fostering rescue dogs, and searching for the world's best margarita.

Novak's work in UDL has impacted educators worldwide as her contributions and collaborations have built upon the founda-tion for an education that is critical for student success. You can connect with her at novakeducation.com or through Twitter and Instagram (@KatieNovakUDL).